The Trojan War in Ancient Art

The Trojan War in Ancient Art

Susan Woodford

Duckworth

First published in 1993 by
Gerald Duckworth & Co. Ltd.
The Old Piano Factory
48 Hoxton Square, London N1 6PB
Tel: 071 729 5986
Fax: 071 729 0015

A catalogue record for this book is available
from the British Library

ISBN 0 7156 2468 7 pbk

Photoset in North Wales by
Derek Doyle & Associates, Mold, Clwyd.
Printed and bound in Great Britain by
The Bath Press, Avon.

Contents

TO JULIA

a bright-eyed listener once, a sharp-eyed critic now.

Preface

Greek myths possess great power and much charm. Greek artists illustrated them with imagination and subtlety, creating works that inspired the culturally docile Romans and remain impressive to this day. It is surprising, therefore, that the attractive subject of mythological iconography has been comparatively neglected; while many books have been devoted either to Greek mythology or to Greek and Roman art, very few have been concerned specifically with the *illustration* of myths.

I have written this book to provide an introduction to the study of mythological illustration in classical antiquity.

I chose to concentrate on the Trojan War because the story has been famous from antiquity until the present day and because it has generated a large and varied body of ancient literature, of which substantial amounts have survived. The Trojan legend provided subject matter for the Homeric epics and the Attic tragedians, for Virgil and Ovid, and for many lesser luminaries, both Greek and Latin. Against such an accessible literary background, the visual images acquire context and gain impact.

The importance of this literary background should not, however, be exaggerated. The illustration of myths in antiquity was something fundamentally different from the illustration of Bible stories in later times. Mythology in antiquity was never formally codified; nor, in fact, was it enshrined in books alone. Tales were also passed on orally from generation to generation and this meant that myths could survive – and even flourish – without fixed texts.

The oral tradition spawned endless variety. There never was a final canon, a definitive version of a myth. The legend of Troy, for instance, was famous long before Homer immortalised small portions of it in the *Iliad* and the *Odyssey*, and later poets felt free to develop well-known incidents, to flesh out hitherto neglected parts of the saga or even to fill in gaps with creations of their own, unfettered by dogma, like Homer himself. Characters were developed and re-evaluated, motivation was constantly analysed and re-interpreted.

What was true for poets was equally true for visual artists. From artists' works – and these are the main concern of this book – we can see that they too felt free to illustrate or expand familiar episodes or to invent new ones. Normally they would follow formulae devised by their predecessors, but occasionally they would create original images of their own, rethinking the implications of a story and presenting personal interpretations that revolutionised the conventional view of the tradition.

Although poets and artists in classical antiquity had much in common, there are fundamental differences between telling a story in words and representing it visually. Words can never be simply translated into images. Artists first had to invent devices that would enable them, within a static scene, to convey the whole sequence of events that made up a story. Only after convincing and widely accepted conventions had been created could artists begin to draw on them routinely, ingeniously modify them or even discard them entirely.

This book examines how artists in classical antiquity went about illustrating the myths of the Trojan War. It is intended to alert readers to the kinds of choices artists have to make, the means they employ to ensure that a story can be correctly identified, the moment in a story that they choose to represent, and the devices they invent to convey the pathos or humour they have discerned in an otherwise hackneyed theme.

Narrating the story of the Trojan War, while drawing on a variety of literary sources and a large range of images, seemed an apt way to introduce the problems faced and the solutions arrived at by Greek and Roman artists when they set about illustrating myths. Since only a small number of the many episodes that cluster around the legend of Troy could be presented, I have chosen those which contribute most to our understanding of mythological illustration. Some readers may regret the omission of one or more favourites – just as I do.

The eight chapters that constitute the heart of the book are supplemented by an epilogue, an appendix and a glossary. The epilogue concludes the story by recounting briefly (without illustrations) events that occurred after the sack of Troy. The appendix provides some art-historical background to the illustrations. Since the illustrations are introduced in an order that is dictated by the course of the story of the Trojan War, without regard to the chronological order in which the works were created, the appendix should help readers to set these works into a more general historical context. The glossary consists of two alphabetical lists, one of real historical persons and the other of mythological characters, each name briefly annotated.

The illustrations have been selected with two points in mind: that they should be intelligible and that they should contribute to the point under discussion. Many potentially relevant Roman paintings have been excluded because they are difficult to decipher in photographs, and several examples of sculpture have been omitted because they did not contribute substantially to the argument in hand or are so damaged that only specialists can interpret their significance. I have included a large number of vase paintings because vase painters were among the most prolific illustrators of myths and often the first to tackle fundamental problems of mythological illustration. Many vases, and even fragments of vases, are quite comprehensible and reveal simply and clearly what these problems were and how they were dealt with.

These choices are, of course, personal, and the selection of stories and images presented in this book is far from comprehensive. My hope is that readers armed with new insights will be tempted to explore this fascinating field further and thereby reap rich rewards both within and beyond the legend of the Trojan War.

I am very grateful to Deborah Blake, Lucilla Burn, Alan Griffiths, Catherine Hobey Hamsher, Ian Jenkins, Carla Lord, Ian McPhee, James Morwood, Olga Palagia, Elizabeth Pemberton, Rowena Rosenbaum, Frances Shaw, Helen Solomon, Dyfri Williams, Peter and Julia Woodford who have taken the trouble to give me their time and valuable criticism, though none are to blame for idiosyncrasies or errors that have persisted despite their scrutiny and advice.

Dyfri Williams kindly suggested that I make use of his restoration of the figure of Ajax in Fig. 93, which Sue Bird has drawn for me. Sue Bird has also lent me the aid of her sharp mind and skilful hand in drawing the map and Figs. 37, 48, 77, and Fig. 59 (after E. Gerhard *Auserlesene griechische Vasenbilder* (Berlin 1847) vol. III, 195-196) and making minor restorations where necessary. Ray Davies has been unstinting of time and effort in producing an attractive lay-out that we hope will be both easy and pleasant to use.

My very special thanks go to Jane Henle whose lively, learned and inspiring course at Columbia University many years ago first introduced me to the joys of mythological iconography. It is the torch she lit that I hope to pass on.

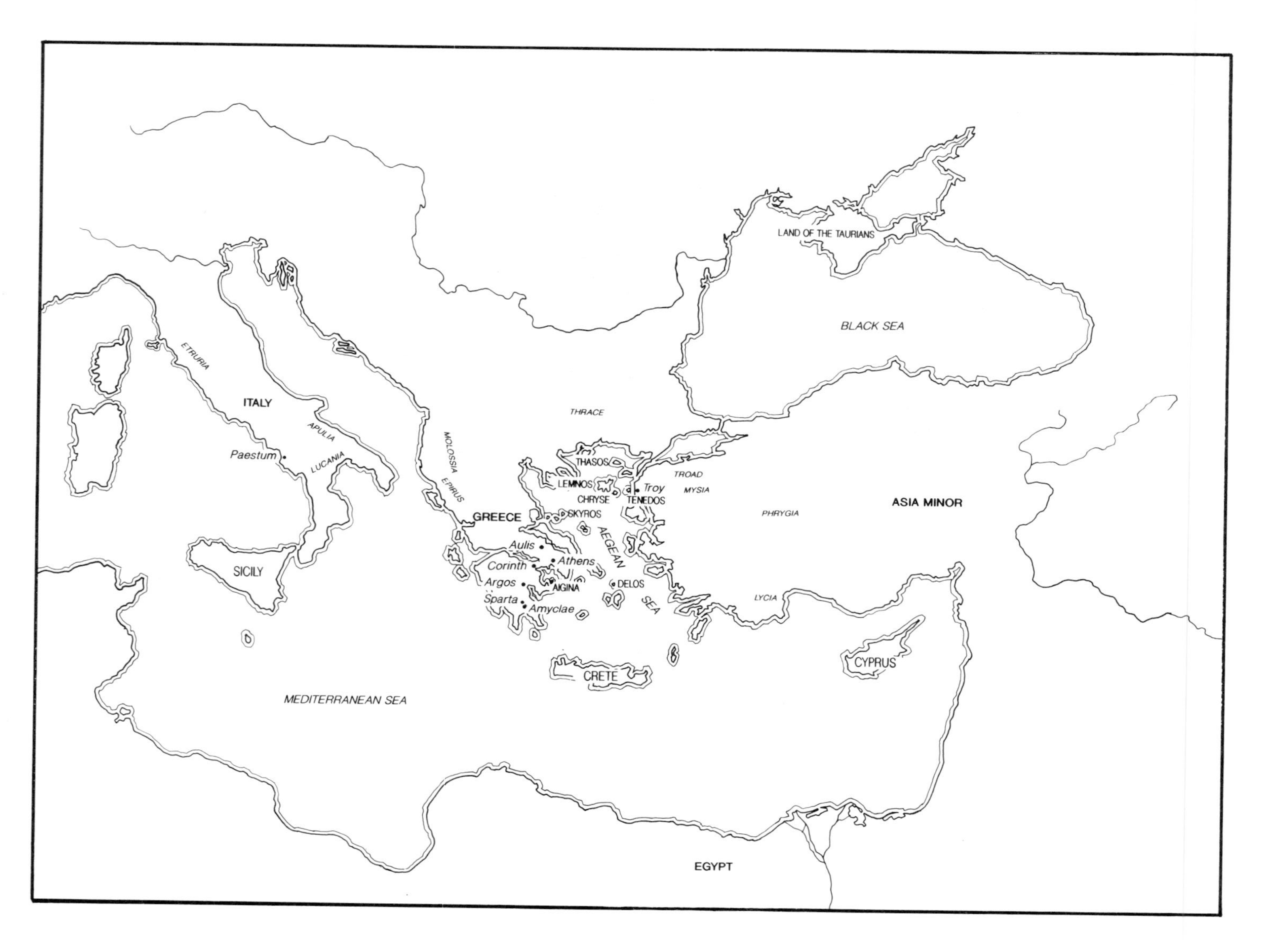
LAND OF THE TAURIANS
BLACK SEA
THRACE
ITALY
ETRURIA
APULIA
LUCANIA
Paestum
MOLOSSIA
EPIRUS
THASOS
LEMNOS
CHRYSE
Troy
TENEDOS
TROAD
MYSIA
PHRYGIA
ASIA MINOR
GREECE
SKYROS
AEGEAN
SEA
Aulis
Athens
Corinth
Argos
AIGINA
DELOS
Sparta
Amyclae
SICILY
LYCIA
CRETE
CYPRUS
MEDITERRANEAN SEA
EGYPT

Acknowledgments

The author and publisher wish to thank all those who have supplied and given permission to reproduce photographs:

Antalya Museum, Turkey, 15
Antikenmuseum Basel, 66, 95
Badisches Landesmuseum Karlsruhe, 10
Susan Bird, 37, 48, 59, 77
Bochum, Ruhr-Universität, 88
British Museum, 3-5, 20, 24, 26, 34, 40, 43, 49, 53, 63, 67, 73-4, 80, 83, 85-6, 101, 105-7, 113
Fratelli Alinari, 21
German Archaeological Institute, Rome, 22
Hirmer Fotoarchiv, Munich, 32, 54-5, 90
Institut National d'Archéologie et d'Art, Tunisia, 31
Kunsthistorisches Museum, Vienna, 39, 92-3, 96
Martin Kestner Museum, Hanover, 14
Martin von Wagner Museum der Universität Würzburg, 64
Master and Fellows of Corpus Christi College, Cambridge, 36
Metropolitan Museum of Art, New York, 45, 68, 72, 97
Musée des Beaux Arts et d'Archéologie, Boulogne-sur-Mer, 16
Musée du Louvre, 17-18, 28, 46, 84, 87
Musei Vaticani, 33, 82, 91, 98
Museo Archeologico di Spina, Ferrara, 30
Museum of Art, Toledo, Ohio, 108
Museum of Fine Arts, Boston, 29, 35, 38, 56-8, 71, 76, 102
National Archaeological Museum, Athens, 44, 75
National Museum, Copenhagen, 78
Soprintendenza Archeologica delle Provincie di Napoli e Caserta – Napoli, 1, 19, 25, 27, 60-2, 99
Soprintendenza Archeologica Etruria Meridionale, 103, 109
Soprintendenza Archeologica per la Toscana – Firenze, 52
Staatliche Antikensammlungen und Glyptothek, Munich, 42, 50, 110
Staatliche Museen Preussischer Kulturbesitz, 11, 23
Professor A.D. Trendall, 47
Susan Woodford, 69

1. The Birth of Helen, Campanian red-figure bell krater, about 340 BC, by the Caivano Painter, Naples, Museo Nazionale.

1

To Begin at the Beginning

One cannot begin the story of the Trojan war with the fighting – or even at Troy itself. To begin at the beginning, one has to start with the egg, or as the Romans put it: *ab ovo*. This was, of course, no ordinary egg. It came into being in the following way.

The chief of the gods, Zeus, had a weakness for pretty women. Leda, wife of Tyndareus, the king of Sparta, was very pretty indeed and Zeus found her quite irresistible. In order to make his affair with her more discreet, Zeus disguised himself as a swan, and in this seductive form he embraced Leda. As a consequence of this union, Leda gave birth to an egg, which, when hatched, revealed no chick or cygnet, but rather a lovely girl – a girl, in fact, of incredible beauty. This was Helen.

When it came to illustrating myths, vase painters living in the Greek cities that had been established in South Italy seem to have been specially blessed with a sense of humour. They were quick to see – and to portray – the funny side of a story. Here is how they imagined the birth of Helen (Fig. 1). The crucial egg sits on an altar. To the left stands Leda, her eyes staring in amazement, one hand lifted in astonishment. To the right, her husband, Tyndareus, takes the event more philosophically, leaning on his staff. But it is, of course, Helen who steals the scene. Small, but perfectly formed, she emerges from the split shell of the egg, arms thrust out in the confident gesture of an acknowledged super-star. One can almost hear the fanfare she expects to greet her. It was her fate to grow up into the most beautiful woman in the world, and she seems to have grasped that fact right from the start.

Beautiful women are lovely to look at, but they can cause a lot of trouble; this was certainly the case with Helen. Perhaps that is why one tradition in antiquity suggested she was not really the daughter of Leda at all, but rather the child of Nemesis (the personification of divine retribution) and that Nemesis gave Helen (possibly while she was still in the egg) to Leda to bring up. In any case, Helen grew up in Leda's family and was accepted by Tyndareus as his daughter.

Helen's beauty was destined to bring death and destruction, and as she grew toward womanhood, Tyndareus could already see that trouble was brewing. When word of Helen's beauty got out, prospective husbands came from far and wide to court her. As the number of rich and powerful suitors increased and as their passions rose in their rivalry, Tyndareus became more and more alarmed. He realised that in selecting a husband for Helen, he would make a friend of one man but would antagonise all the rest. He feared violence.

One of Helen's more modest suitors was Odysseus. He came from the rocky island of Ithaca and was neither very rich nor very powerful. He had little hope of winning Helen, and in any case he really had his heart set on Penelope, Tyndareus' niece. What he lacked in wealth Odysseus made up for in cleverness, and he offered to help Tyndareus out of his dilemma provided Tyndareus helped him win Penelope. Tyndareus agreed. Odysseus advised Tyndareus to make the suitors swear a solemn oath that they would under all circumstances uphold and defend Helen's husband, whoever he might be, and that Helen should then choose the lucky man herself. Tyndareus was delighted with the suggestion and adopted it at once.

Helen chose Menelaos, whose brother was Agamemnon, mighty king of rich Mycenae. Menelaos was a handsome and wealthy man and a creditable warrior, but he was not strikingly intelligent or perceptive, as subsequent events were to prove.

2. Peleus and Thetis, Attic red-figure cup interior, about 500 BC, by Peithinos, Berlin, Charlottenburg.

*

Some time after the marriage of Helen and Menelaos, Peleus and Thetis were wed. This was a far more spectacular event, for Thetis was a Nereid, a sea-goddess, and her wedding was celebrated on a grand scale – not by ordinary human beings, but by immortal gods and goddesses. This may have been in part to console Thetis for a marriage that she considered rather beneath her. Her husband, Peleus, was a mere mortal and she was, at first, very reluctant to become his wife.

Being a sea-creature, Thetis had the ability to change her shape into anything she chose. When Peleus came to woo her she resisted him by turning herself first into a roaring lion, then into a hissing snake and finally into flowing water and burning fire. These last two were especially difficult to get a grip on, but Peleus held on undeterred, showing himself to be a man of great determination, and in the end Thetis relented, resumed her normal shape and consented to marry him.

The transformations of Thetis are easily evoked by poets, but they are difficult for an artist to convey in a static picture. One way of dealing with the problem was to depict Thetis in her true form, that is, as a lovely sea-nymph, but at the same time to *hint* at her transformations by means of subsidiary figures. Sometimes these could be panthers or sea-monsters. In Fig. 2 Peleus firmly grasps Thetis around the waist. Three snakes (one held by Thetis, another wound about Peleus' arms and a third looped around one calf and nipping his heel) and a small lion (which appears to be climbing down Peleus' back) symbolise Thetis' metamorphoses. Peleus' tenacity is revealed in the way his hands are clasped together: so firmly are his fingers intertwined that they are locked into a geometric pattern.

If we did not already know the story, this image would be baffling. We might, however, be tempted to *invent* a story to go with the picture and then imagine that the picture illustrated that very invention – a neat piece of circular reasoning. The Greeks themselves may well have done

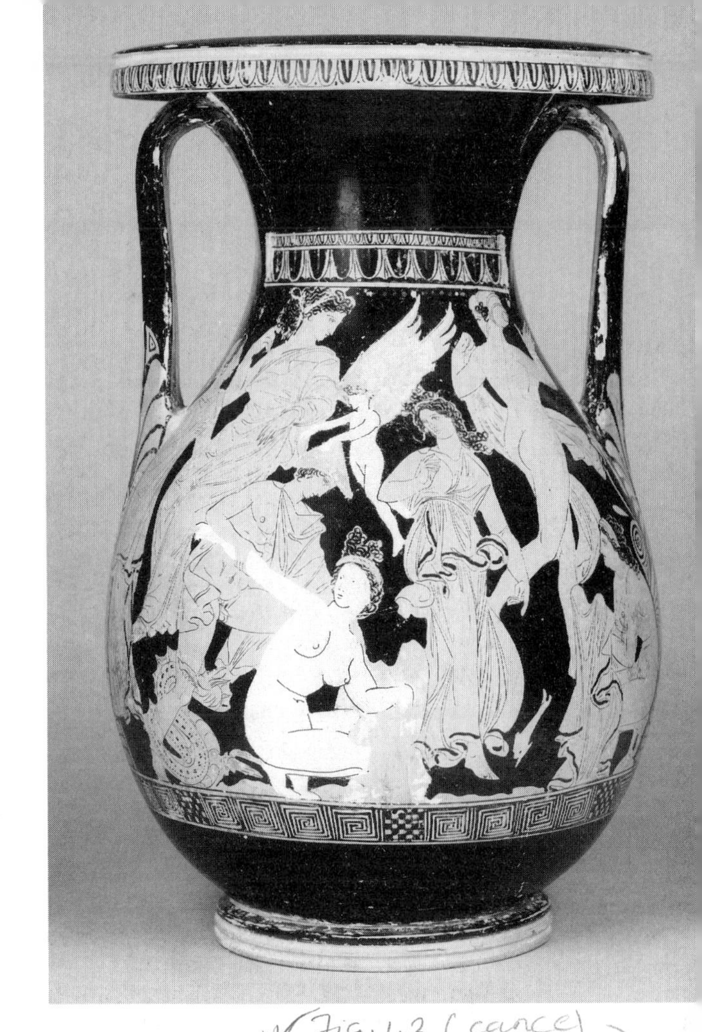

3. Peleus and Thetis, Attic red-figure pelike (Kerch style), about 350 BC, by the Marsyas Painter, London, British Museum.

this when they began to import objects from foreign countries. These objects often portrayed interesting-looking subjects, but they arrived without labels or explanations, and the Greeks had no idea what they represented in the minds of the people who had created them. The Greeks made up stories to explain the images, but neither they nor we could decipher the original story from the image alone. It should always be remembered that it is impossible for us to interpret illustrations of unknown myths; otherwise, we may fall into the seductive trap of imposing stories that are modern inventions on hitherto unexplained ancient images.

No rules dictated to any artist in antiquity exactly how a myth had to be portrayed in either words or pictures. Thus, while some painters liked to show Peleus overcoming all obstacles to claim his bride, others preferred to focus on a different aspect of the story. The painter of Fig. 3, for instance, preferred to stress the amorous conclusion of the encounter. He has spotlighted Thetis, painted white, crouching in the foreground about to bathe, when Peleus (to the left) suddenly seizes her. A small sea-monster winding around Peleus' right leg hints at Thetis' transformations, but the emphasis of the picture is on the ultimate triumph of love, indicated by the white-painted love-god, Eros, who flies down to crown Peleus, and the goddess of love herself, Aphrodite, seated above and to the left of Peleus. The rest of the scene is mostly filled by Thetis' sister-Nereids; they were numerous and affectionate and much concerned with Thetis' fate.

The two topmost figures are depicted in a way that makes brilliant use of the curving shape of the vase they decorate: the one to the left, Aphrodite, is seated comfortably, actually leaning against the curve of the vase. The startled Nereid on the right – alarmed by Peleus' unexpected intrusion on the scene – is shown in back view, fleeing. Her extraordinarily elegant form is perfectly adjusted to the undulating surface of the vessel.

Once Peleus had caught his bride, he was free to marry her. The wedding was celebrated with great pomp, as Thetis was popular among the gods, and they wished to do her honour. The top row of figures decorating a bowl (Figs. 4-5) is devoted to a depiction of the wedding guests arriving at the house of Peleus. Peleus (Fig. 4) stands before the closed door (we must imagine Thetis discreetly hidden behind it) hospitably proffering a cup of wine. He is approached by Iris (a messenger of the gods, who wears a short skirt so that she can run more easily) leading four goddesses, all carefully

4. The Wedding of Peleus and Thetis: Peleus receives the guests, including Cheiron, Attic black-figure dinos (mixing bowl), about 580 BC, by Sophilos, London, British Museum.

5. The Wedding of Peleus and Thetis: Gods arriving in chariots (the other side of Fig. 4).

labelled for easy identification and elaborately dressed in splendidly embroidered robes. Next comes the wine-god, Dionysos, carrying part of a flourishing vine, followed by Hebe, the goddess of youth – both highly desirable guests. After them comes Cheiron, a centaur, a mythical creature who is part man and part horse. Other centaurs were crude, rough fellows, but Cheiron was exceptional in being both wise and cultured. Four more goddesses follow on foot, while round the other side of the bowl (Fig. 5) more deities arrive, some, like Zeus and his wife Hera, riding grandly in four-horse chariots. The figures are mostly drawn in black on the shiny orange surface of the bowl and enlivened with touches of white and purplish-red. Internal markings, when not painted, are delicately incised, clearly distinguishing one horse from another in what otherwise might be a tangle of overlapping forms, and carefully delineating neatly trimmed beards and finely waved hair.

The decorous behaviour of the invited guests would seem to have boded well for the success of the party, but this did not take into account the feelings of the one *uninvited* guest: Eris, the goddess of discord. Her presence and the sort of effect she produced on others were considered to be undesirable. This point seemed obvious to everybody, except, of course, Eris herself, who like any bad fairy – or ordinary person, for that matter – was insulted to have been left out. Invited or not, Eris put in an appearance,

6. Eris (Discord), Attic black-figure cup interior, about 560 BC, Berlin, Charlottenburg.

and into the midst of the assembly she tossed a golden apple. On it were written the words: 'For the Fairest.'

We shall return in a moment to this apple of discord and the turmoil it caused, but first we should consider what an abstract concept like 'discord' might look like. Poets have little difficulty sketching in the complex overtones associated with such a personification, but these are more difficult to convey in a visual image. In fact, Eris was seldom portrayed. Pausanias, who lived in the 2nd century AD, says that he saw her represented between two duelling warriors, on an elaborately decorated chest made some seven or eight hundred years before his time. She was, he said, very ugly. The chest no longer exists and only a few images of Eris still survive. Fig. 6 is a rare early picture of her, made not long after the one that Pausanias saw. Here she does not look very terrible – just a winged female figure in a hurry. An image of Victory (another personification) would not look very different. One could hardly guess that Eris' intention was to make trouble, were it not for the fact that her name is written beneath her.

But Eris lived up to her name, and the apple produced just the sort of discord she had desired. Greek goddesses were as vain as mortal women, and more than one of them was tempted by the golden apple that purported to be the prize for beauty. Nevertheless, only three formidable goddesses actually dared to claim it: Hera, the wife of Zeus, Athena, his daughter, and Aphrodite, the goddess of love. Zeus was too clever to allow himself to be lured into the role of judge, for it was clear that although one goddess could be satisfied, the other two would be fiercely resentful. It was equally clear, however, that something had to be done. Zeus therefore summoned Hermes, the messenger god, and instructed him to take the three contending goddesses to the Trojan prince Paris and have him judge the winner. Paris was, at that time, temporarily

acting as a herdsman on Mount Ida.

Vase painters in antiquity loved to illustrate the Judgement of Paris. They enjoyed the challenge of having to produce a handsome piece of decoration while at the same time conveying the gist of the story. Different artists approached the task in different ways. In Fig. 7 an Athenian vase painter in the early 6th century BC portrayed the three competing goddesses as virtually indistinguishable. Their identical figures, each wearing much the same kind of clothing, each standing in the same pose, each holding a wreath, produce a repeated pattern not very different from that of the decorative leaves in the border above them. Their staid forms in a static compact group contrast with the activity of Hermes, vigorously striding out to overtake Paris and inform him of the task before him. Paris, at the far right, depicted as a mature man with a beard, clutches his lyre and prudently takes to his heels.

An Etruscan vase painter, a little later, found quite another way to decorate his vase while telling the same story (Fig. 8). Instead of bunching his goddesses together, he has spread them out. They are led, as usual, by Hermes, and he is preceded by an old man, whose identity is by no means clear. (Is he a local herald?

7. *Above* The Judgement of Paris, Attic black-figure amphora, about 575-550 BC, Paris, Louvre.

8. The Judgement of Paris, Pontic amphora (Etruscan black-figure), about 530 BC, by the Paris Painter, Munich, Antikensammlungen.

9. The Judgement of Paris, Attic red-figure cup exterior, 490-480 BC, by Makron, Berlin, Staatliche Antikensammlungen.

He holds a herald's staff, but there is nothing in the story, as it is usually told, to explain his presence.) The five figures are evenly spaced to give a series of regular accents, but each one is vividly differentiated from the other. Not only is Hermes, beardless and dark-haired, distinguished from his elderly white-haired companion by the style and decoration of his clothing, but the three goddesses also are characterised highly individually. Hera comes first, identifiable by the bridal gesture of lifting her veil. She is followed by Athena, a warrior goddess holding her spear. Finally, climactically, Aphrodite approaches. She wears an elegant snood over her hair and a fashionable pair of shoes with up-turned toes. The rustic Paris is represented on the other side of the vase with his herd.

A third example, from the beginning of the 5th century BC (Fig. 9), illustrates yet another, perhaps subtler, manner of portraying the story. A youthful, beardless Paris is seated at the left, playing the lyre while tending his flocks, when Hermes approaches him leading the three goddesses. Powerful Athena, armed with her helmet and spear and wearing her aegis (a snake-trimmed scaly sort of poncho) comes first, making a gesture as if she were about to speak. Queenly Hera, holding a sceptre, comes next, while demurely-veiled Aphrodite, surrounded by fluttering little love gods, comes last. She, too, makes a gesture as if she were about to speak. The tradition actually does suggest that the goddesses were not content simply to have Paris judge them on the merits of their looks, but – just to make sure – tried to influence him by the offer of attractive bribes. Hera offered him lordship over a wide empire, Athena offered invincible prowess in war, and Aphrodite offered the possession of the most beautiful woman in the world. This last proved irresistible, and Paris gave her the apple.

The consequences proved dire, but before we follow them up, let us look at one last example of the way a vase painter could illustrate the story. The three vases we have looked at so far, despite their diversity, have one thing in common: all three show the goddesses being led in procession in order to be judged. Toward the end of the 5th century BC the painter

10. The Judgement of Paris, Attic red-figure hydria, about 420-400 BC, by the Painter of the Carlsruhe Paris, Karlsruhe, Badisches Landesmuseum.

of Fig. 10 arranged the scene quite differently. There is no procession. In fact, at first glance it is difficult to see that we are even dealing with the same subject. Lots of women seem to be present and it takes some time to work out exactly who is to be judged and who is doing the judging. An elaborately dressed, trousered figure sits in the centre with a dog beside him. This is Paris; his special costume identifies him as a Trojan and his dog shows that he is a herdsman. A little Eros stands at his shoulder, no doubt trying to influence his decision. To the right we can recognise Hermes by his herald's staff. He is young and beardless, a characterisation preferred in the late 5th century BC. To the left of Paris, we can recognise Athena armed with her spear, wearing her helmet and aegis and carrying a shield. A little below her and to the left stands Hera, lifting her veil and holding her sceptre. One searches among the remaining female figures for Aphrodite, only to find her confidently seated just to the right of Hermes with another Eros by her side. The other figures, like the principals, are labelled, but few of them are as germane to the story as Eris, whose upper body appears just above Paris as she peers over the edge of a hillock at the consequences of her scheming. This quiet scene illustrates the stillness before the storm. Such pictures, lacking in explicit action but pregnant with meaning, began to come into fashion in the second quarter of the 5th century

BC along with the arrangement of relatively small figures placed at different heights rather than large figures simply disposed along a single ground line. These compositional and emotional innovations probably resulted from the influence of a famous mural painter, Polygnotos, whose highly original works (now lost) inspired vase painters to try to follow his lead.

Like painters, poets felt free to approach the story of the Judgement of Paris from different angles and to interpret it in different ways. The comical idea that proud goddesses would hastily invent seductive bribes in order to win a token prize for beauty particularly appealed to the 2nd century AD satirist Lucian and he set about evoking the scene verbally. He portrayed Paris as quite dazzled by the majesty of the goddesses, but still retaining enough presence of mind to request them to present themselves in the full splendour of their naked beauty. Each goddess contrived to have a private word with him. This is what Aphrodite said when she was briefly alone with Paris:

> 'Here I am; take your time and examine carefully; let nothing escape your vigilance. And I have something else to say to you, handsome Paris. Yes, you handsome boy, I have long had an eye on you; I think you must be the handsomest young fellow in all Phrygia [the area around Troy]. But it is such a pity that you don't leave these rocks and crags, and live in a town: you will lose all your beauty in this desert. What have you to do with mountains? What satisfaction can your beauty give to a lot of cows? You ought to have been married long ago; not to any of those dowdy women hereabouts, but to some Greek girl; an Argive, perhaps, or a Corinthian, or a Spartan; Helen, now, is a Spartan, and such a pretty girl – quite as pretty as I am – and so susceptible! Why, if she once caught sight of *you*, she would give up everything, I am sure, to go with you, and a most devoted wife she would be. But you have heard of Helen, of course?'

Paris had not heard of Helen and Aphrodite explains:

> 'Well, she is the daughter of Leda, the beautiful woman, you know, whom Zeus visited in the disguise of a swan. ... She is fair, as might be expected from the swan, soft as down (she was hatched from an egg, you know) and such a lithe, graceful figure ... when she grew up, the very first men in Greece were suitors for her hand, and she was given to Menelaos... Now, if you like, she shall be your wife.'

Naïve Paris is dismayed by the fact that Helen is already married and doubts that she would give up everything for him, but Aphrodite reassures him:

> '... I have two beautiful children, Love and Desire. They shall be your guides. Love will assail her in all his might, and compel her to love you: Desire will encompass you about, and make you desirable and lovely as himself; and I will be there to help. I can get the Graces to come too, and between us we shall prevail.'
>
> Lucian *Dialogues of the Gods* 20, 13-16
> (trans. Fowler and Fowler)

Paris is persuaded, overwhelmed, intoxicated. In exchange for the promise of Helen, he gives the apple to Aphrodite.

While Lucian enjoyed elaborating a story that had been well known for centuries, other authors tell the tale more briefly or merely allude to it. The 5th century BC tragic poet Euripides does this in several plays, though on one occasion he does not simply recall the story, but has one of his characters actually refute it. In his play *The Trojan Women*, Hekabe, the aged and grieving queen of fallen Troy, denies that there ever was a Judgement of Paris, for, she claims:

> 'I do not believe that Hera and virgin Athena were ever so silly that the one was ready to barter away Argos [a city in Greece supposed to be dear to Hera] to the barbarians, the other to make her Athens the slave of Phrygia, and all for a

11. Menelaos receives Paris and Aeneas in the presence of Helen, Attic red-figure cup exterior, 440-430 BC, by the Painter of Berlin 2536, Berlin, Charlottenburg.

childish whim that took them to Ida to quarrel about their beauty. For why should goddess Hera have conceived such a passion for beauty? Did she hope to get a better husband than Zeus? Was Athena laying her lines for a match with one of the gods, Athena who shuns wedlock and begged the Father to let her remain a virgin?'

Euripides *Trojan Women* 971-981
(trans. Hadas and McLean)

Such was the flexibility of the Greek mythological tradition that it allowed not only for modification and elaboration, but even for contradiction.

Nevertheless, the generally accepted tale was that the contest took place, Aphrodite was awarded the apple and the two other goddesses retired outraged, never to forgive Paris.

*

12. Aphrodite persuades Helen to elope with Paris, Attic red-figure pointed amphoriskos, about 430 BC, by the Heimarmene Painter, Berlin, Staatliche Antikensammlungen.

13. Helen elopes with Paris, Attic red-figure skyphos, 490-480 BC, by Makron, Boston, Museum of Fine Arts.

Aphrodite had promised Helen to Paris, and now she had to make good her word. She helped Paris to arrange a visit to Greece and sent her own son Aeneas, who was Paris' cousin, along with him. At Sparta, Menelaos received the Trojan visitors hospitably, but then was called away to attend a relative's funeral in Crete. He left Helen in charge of entertaining their guests.

A 5th-century BC vase painter (Fig. 11) shows Menelaos greeting Paris and Aeneas, while Helen, seated, sensing a threat, turns away. Eros, the love god, is already at her feet – and the coercion promised by Aphrodite looms.

However virtuous she may have tried to be, the odds were against Helen. How could she withstand the blandishments of Aphrodite, who was ready to plead in person for Paris? This point is made by another 5th century BC vase painter (Fig. 12). Aphrodite is shown holding Helen on her lap. Helen, her chin in her hand, is pensive and withdrawn. Paris stands to the right with a winged boy beside him. The youth looks like Eros, the god of love, but he is labelled 'Himeros' (Desire). Another of Aphrodite's attendants stands to the left, carrying a jewel box. She is labelled 'Peitho' (Persuasion). Firmly held by Aphrodite, trapped between Desire and Persuasion, Helen has little hope of escaping her fate. The point is underlined by the inclusion of two further personifications: 'Heimarmene' (Destiny) is present to the right, turning her back on Paris to address an unidentified woman with a bird on one hand, while Nemesis, at the far left, leans on the shoulder of a woman whose label is no longer intelligible, and points a finger at the lovers-to-be. Clearly retribution is already waiting in the wings.

Of course Helen went to Troy with Paris. A beautiful early 5th century BC vase (Fig. 13) shows Aeneas leading the way, while Paris follows, looking lovingly back at Helen and holding her by the wrist – a ritual gesture used in marriage ceremonies in Athens at the time when the vase was painted. Helen, veiled, is led on by Eros, encouraged by Aphrodite, who reaches forward to adjust Helen's veil and send her on her way, while Peitho (Persuasion), her task completed, raises one hand in farewell.

These vases seem to suggest that Helen was the passive victim of Aphrodite, blameless herself but unable to avoid being manipulated by the goddess. This appears to have been the view of Homer, the poet who composed the *Iliad* and the *Odyssey*, probably during the 8th century BC. Only once in the *Iliad* does Helen attempt to assert her own will and defy Aphrodite. This show of independence is instantly quashed. Aphrodite grows angry; her terrible power becomes manifest. Helen is rightly frightened and meekly does what she is told. She cannot stand up against the might of the goddess.

But Euripides often painted quite a different picture of Helen. In *The Trojan Women* he has Helen defend her elopement with Paris by means of transparently sophistic arguments. Among other things, she claims that Aphrodite herself (or 'Cypris', as she sometimes calls her) accompanied Paris and coerced her. Euripides makes Hekabe see through her excuses and call her briskly to account:

> 'Don't make the gods silly to cover up your own wickedness,' she says, 'You'll find you cannot convince the wise. And Cypris – this is very funny – you say she came with my son to the home of Menelaos. Could she not have stayed quietly in heaven and brought you, Amyclae and all to Ilium?* My son was of surpassing beauty; at the sight of him your heart transformed itself into Cypris. Every lewd impulse in man passes for Aphrodite. ... So when you saw my son in the splendour of gold and barbaric raiment, mad desire took possession of your heart. In Argos† you were used to a small retinue; having got rid of the Spartan city, you looked forward to a deluge of extravagance in Phrygia with its rivers of gold. The halls of Menelaos weren't large enough for your luxury to wanton in.'
>
> Euripides *Trojan Women* 981-997
> (trans. Hadas and McLean)

This unlovely picture of Helen appears in most of Euripides' extant tragedies, but there is one exception: *Helen*. In *Helen*, the heroine is vindicated. She is not only exonerated from willingly having gone to Troy; she is proved never to have gone at all! Instead, according to Euripides – and some other poets before him – although she was forced to leave Sparta with Paris, when they landed in Egypt she stayed there and only a phantom in her shape went on to Troy. The war, with all its wretchedness and bloodshed, was, therefore, simply fought over an illusion. Helen preserved her virtue (if not her reputation) throughout.

Consistency and logic are not the outstanding qualities of the Greek mythological tradition; instead, its flexibility allows for constant creative renewal and re-interpretation, infinitely rich and inspiring.

* Amyclae was a sanctuary near Sparta, here meant to stand for the city itself. Ilium was another name for Troy.

† The poet seems here to be locating Helen's home of Sparta in Argos.

2

The Army Assembles

When Menelaos returned home from Crete to discover that Helen had been carried off by Paris, he recalled to the suitors the oath they had all taken when he had married Helen and reminded them that now the time had come for them to rally to his aid.

The army that assembled in response to his summons was thus composed chiefly of Helen's suitors, bound by oath to support her husband; but to this rule there were two notable exceptions: Agamemnon and Achilles.

Agamemnon, Menelaos' powerful brother, had not been among Helen's suitors – he had already married Helen's sister Klytaimnestra – and he was therefore not obliged to take part in the expedition. Regard for his family's honour and the desire for glory, however, compelled him to join. As king of rich Mycenae, Agamemnon was immensely wealthy and was able to contribute more ships and men than any other ruler. This fact, combined with his relationship to the aggrieved Menelaos, no doubt enabled him to claim the role of commander-in-chief. Homer portrayed him as well qualified – on the whole – for his exalted position, his usually dignified and regal demeanour only occasionally marred by his hot temper or anxious indecision. Euripides, by contrast, felt free to paint an ugly picture of him, depicting him currying favour with all and sundry, like the lowest kind of scheming politician, in order to gain power and prestige.

If it seems odd that the commander-in-chief of the Greek army defending the honour of Helen's chosen husband had not been among Helen's suitors, it is odder yet that the man who was to become the most formidable fighter in the whole Greek army had not been among them either. This was Achilles. Although he had not even been born at the time when Helen's hand was being sued for, his destiny eventually came to be inseparably entwined with hers.

Achilles was the son of Peleus and Thetis, the very couple whose wedding had been disrupted by Eris and the golden apple.

Thetis had been pained by the idea that she, a goddess, should have to bear a mortal child who was fated to die. She therefore tried to remedy the situation. Traditions vary as to how she set about this, but all agree that her efforts proved only partially successful. One tradition suggests that Thetis endeavoured to burn away the infant Achilles' mortality in a fire (or in boiling water) but that she was caught in the act by Peleus, who, understandably dismayed when he witnessed a procedure that seemed monstrously cruel, cried out in horror. Thetis, enraged by his interference, threw the baby down on the ground and, leaving the job unfinished, departed in disgust for her father's house under the sea.

Another, rather later tradition claims that Thetis tried to protect her son by dipping him in the running waters of the

14. Thetis dipping Achilles in the Styx, Sard, possibly 1st century BC, Hanover, Kestner Museum.

Styx, the river of the Underworld. She held him by one ankle (Figs. 14 and 15) and succeeded in making him invulnerable in all the parts of his body that were touched by the water. But the ankle by which she held him remained dry – with fatal consequences. Homer eschews both traditions. In the *Iliad*, he portrays Achilles as a brave warrior, one whose courage is not compromised by reliance on any magic protection.

Thetis' attempts to make her son immortal did not appeal to Greek artists. None of them showed her burning away her son's mortality in fire or curing it in boiling water, and only toward the end of the Hellenistic period may a few have begun to represent Thetis dipping Achilles in the Styx. Fig 14 is among the earliest of such images. This small gem is very sensitively executed with the composition beautifully designed to fit into the oval shape, but despite its elegance, it reveals the difficulties inherent in the illustration of this subject.

Thetis kneels gracefully on the bank of the river, grasping Achilles by one ankle, while the baby hangs, limbs dangling helplessly, over the water. Thetis' gesture seems a heartless one; in fact, such a gesture was frequently used in earlier art to indicate a cruel purpose: in images of the fall of Troy (Figs. 101 and 102), a warrior holds an infant callously by the foot ready to dash him to his death. Clearly it was difficult to impart any sense of tenderness to Thetis' action, no matter how finely it was portrayed, and the visual associations with the earlier murderous motif did not make matters easier.

In Roman times, the tradition that Thetis dipped Achilles in the Styx became generally accepted and the incident became a standard part of biographical cycles representing the life of Achilles. For many later artists the dipping of Achilles was nothing more than a conventional image and they made little effort to mitigate its appearance of harsh insensitivity. A crude mosaic (Fig. 15) from the Roman period makes the scene look distressingly violent, but the labelling of 'Thetis', 'Achilles' and 'pege' (the 'running waters' of the Styx) assures its identification.

As Achilles grew older, thought had to be given to his education, and it was decided that he ought to be entrusted to the most distinguished tutor of the day.

15. Thetis dipping Achilles in the Styx, Roman mosaic (from Xanthos), 5th century AD, Antalya Museum (Turkey).

This personage turned out to be the centaur Cheiron, one of the more unusual guests to attend the wedding of Peleus and Thetis (Fig. 4).

Cheiron was in every way unusual. His parents were different from those of the other centaurs and so were his temperament and endowments. In principle, a centaur ought to combine the strength and swiftness of a horse with the intelligence and moral sensibility of a man, but in practice only Cheiron lived up to the full potential. His unique qualities made him seem an ideal tutor for young heroes, and many of the most celebrated were supposed to have profited from his tutelage. Cheiron's physical constitution made him extraordinarily well suited to instruct his young charges in matters of hunting and riding and he was also able to teach them how to fight. Among his more surprising qualifications was his knowledge of music and medicine, both of which he also imparted to his pupils.

According to Greek vase painters, Peleus took responsibility for handing over his little son to the wise centaur. Thetis appears only occasionally, usually in a subordinate role. Some artists suggested that at the time Achilles was still an infant, so small that he had to be carried either in his father's hand (Fig. 16) or in that of the kindly centaur (Fig. 17). Others imagined him to be an older boy, capable of standing on his own two feet (Fig. 18).

Centaurs, being part horse and part man, are imaginary monsters who could not possibly exist in the real world. The two parts of which they were composed could, therefore, be portrayed in any number of combinations, no one of which could be argued to be 'more correct' than another. In actuality they were normally represented in only two ways: either as human down to the waist and below that, horse (Fig. 19) or as fully human in front, with the horse part attached behind the buttocks (Figs. 4, 16-18). The former type seems more 'natural', if one can say such

16. Peleus hands the infant Achilles over to Cheiron, Attic black-figure amphora, about 520 BC, Boulogne-sur-Mer, Musée des Beaux-Arts et d'Archéologie.

17. Cheiron holding the infant Achilles, Attic red-figure amphora, about 520-510 BC, by Oltos, Paris, Louvre.

18. Peleus introduces the young Achilles to Cheiron, Attic red-figure stamnos, about 490 BC, by the Berlin Painter, Paris, Louvre.

a thing about a composite monster. The man-legged type of centaur presents problems logically – for instance, how can his front legs keep up with his back legs when he is running, the horse being so much stronger and faster than the human? Furthermore, if he is shown naked, he has an overabundance of genitals (possessing both a human and an equine set), but if he is clothed, the tailoring problems are considerable. In Fig. 4 Cheiron wears a short tunic, appropriate for a hunter, but in Figs. 16-18, when he is receiving his young pupil, he is clothed in more dignified tutorial robes. In Figs. 16 and 18, his cloak covers his human body in front and is draped over his horse part behind, but the artist of Fig. 17 simply swathed the human part of Cheiron all about with his cloak, leaving the matter of how his horse part might be attached something of a mystery.

A nude, horse-legged type of Cheiron was far easier to handle plausibly. Greek artists may at first have wished to distinguish Cheiron as a man-legged centaur in order to stress his humane character, but with the increasing emphasis on natural appearances in art, they began to depict him as a horse-legged centaur. This was the standard type for the Romans (Fig. 19).

In the Roman wall painting (Fig. 19), which seems to have been copied from a lost Greek prototype, Cheiron, seated rather clumsily on the ground, offers serious instruction in lyre-playing to the young Achilles.

Such a horse-legged type of Cheiron was particularly suitable for instruction in riding. The writer Philostratos describes a painting from the Roman period (now lost) in which this potential is put to full use. In the painting, he says, Cheiron is shown

> teaching Achilles to ride horseback and to use him exactly as a horse, and he measures his gait to what the boy can endure, and turning round he smiles at the boy when he laughs aloud with enjoyment ...
>
> Philostratos (the Elder)
> *Imagines* II, 2, (343K)
> (trans. Fairbanks)

*

Achilles' period of training with Cheiron was cut short by the looming threat of the Trojan war. Thetis knew that Achilles' destiny was either to live a short but glorious life or a long but undistinguished one. If Achilles were to participate in the Trojan campaign, he would surely prove to be a magnificent fighter, but in consequence of this he would die young. Anxious to save her darling son, Thetis snatched Achilles away from Cheiron and looked about for a safe place to conceal the boy from the Greeks whose business it was to persuade heroes to join the enterprise, and who had heard of his brilliant promise.

Achilles was still a beardless youth and Thetis had the ingenious idea of disguising him as a girl and concealing him

19. Cheiron instructs Achilles in playing the lyre, Roman wall painting (copy, presumably, of a Hellenistic Greek prototype), 1st century AD, Naples, Museo Nazionale, from the Basilica at Herculaneum.

among the numerous daughters of Lykomedes, king of Skyros.

When dressed like the girls, Achilles became indistinguishable from them – though an amorous impulse led him to reveal his true nature to one of them, Deidamia, who as a result became the mother of his son Neoptolemos.

The Greeks, recruiting energetically for their expedition, received a prophecy that Troy could not be taken without the aid of Achilles. Rumour led them to the island of Skyros, but they were puzzled as to how to identify Achilles, or at least how to do it without causing intolerable embarrassment all round.

Quick-witted Odysseus, who had given such helpful advice to Tyndareus, was once again able to devise a clever scheme to solve the problem. He sailed to Skyros with his friend Diomedes, both disguised as merchants. The girls, Achilles among them, gathered round as they spread their dainty wares before them. In the midst of the tempting feminine trifles, they placed a spear and shield. The girls – and Achilles among them – ignored the arms. But Odysseus had been ready for this. He had brought a trumpeter along with him, and when he gave the signal, the trumpeter sounded the alarm. The frightened girls rushed about in confusion, but Achilles, his true nature breaking irrepressibly to the surface, seized the spear and shield ready to defy all comers.

Thus Achilles was identified, to nobody's particular embarrassment except Deidamia's – and in her case revelation could not have been delayed much longer anyway. His spirit having

20. Achilles reveals himself (Discovery of Achilles) among the daughters of Lykomedes, part of a Roman sarcophagus, about AD 200-250, London, British Museum.

21. Discovery of Achilles among the daughters of Lykomedes, Roman wall painting, 1st century AD, Naples, Museo Nazionale, from Pompeii.

been roused, Achilles was now easily persuaded to join the expedition against Troy.

Ancient writers tell us that the discovery of Achilles among the daughters of Lykomedes on Skyros was illustrated in a painting as early as the 5th century BC, but all surviving images appear to date from the Roman period. Part of a 3rd century AD sarcophagus (Fig. 20) shows Achilles still dressed like a girl, seizing the spear and the shield, his identity betrayed not by his appearance, but by his character.

An even more excited scene is depicted in a Roman painting (Fig. 21). Achilles' drapery slips from his body as he reaches for the shield. In the same moment, Diomedes, behind him, and Odysseus (wearing the hat that became his usual attribute in art) to the right, seize him. In the left foreground a woman rushes off in such dismay that she loses her grip on her clothing and her delicate nude body is revealed. It contrasts with the rugged form of Achilles, part of the painter's dramatic plan. The scene is crowded with startled women; eager soldiers appear in the background; King Lykomedes is visible in the centre, just behind Achilles. In the upper left corner can be glimpsed the trumpeter whose blast aroused all this confusion and resolved the problem of identifying Achilles.

The decoration on the shield shows Achilles' education at the hands of Cheiron, the very composition that we saw in Fig. 19. This suggests that there once existed a famous image – most probably originally created by a Greek artist – which served as the prototype from which both Fig. 19 and the device on the shield were derived. Roman artists deeply admired the inventions of their Greek predecessors and were proud to copy or adapt them. Some sort of copy-books must have circulated among the Roman craftsmen containing visual formulae that they could use when they were called upon to illustrate popular themes. These could provide inspiration for the gifted, and guidance for the more humble workmen. We can trace their influence in numerous paintings, mosaics, reliefs and even statues, all of which rely on the same basic composition.

This is true not only of the details, but also of the whole of this painting of the discovery of Achilles (Fig. 21), for it is found in several versions, some in painting, others in mosaic (Fig. 22). Some of them are finer than others, with more convincing movement and emotion, but all display the same composition for the main figures. Thus on the mosaic (Fig. 22), Achilles (in the centre) grasping the shield, the startled woman flanking him on the left and the clever Odysseus on the right are all easily recognisable and the same decoration appears on the shield – a sort of quotation within a quotation.

Not all authors agreed that Achilles had to be winkled out of hiding among the daughters of Lykomedes. Homer, for

22. Discovery of Achilles among the daughters of Lykomedes, mosaic, 1st century AD, House of Apollo, Pompeii.

instance, chose to portray Achilles unhesitatingly joining an expedition that he thought would bring him glory, setting out with dignity from his father's house. (According to this version of the story, Achilles fathered his son on Skyros during a stop-over on that island which involved no disguise.)

In any case, Achilles was still very young when he joined the Trojan campaign. Some older companions were therefore sent along with him, among them Phoinix, who was almost like a father to Achilles, and Patroklos – only marginally Achilles' senior – who was his most beloved friend.

*

Once Achilles' participation had been secured, the Greeks were ready to start, but it turned out that they had only the haziest idea of where Troy actually was. They sailed off boldly in roughly the right direction, but landed rather too far to the south in the land of Mysia, ruled over by Telephos. The startled inhabitants, subjected to an unexpected attack from an army suddenly disembarking on their shores, defended themselves courageously. Patroklos proved himself a valiant squire to Achilles and was probably wounded in this fray. This may be why, according to the poet Pindar, Achilles required him henceforth never to fight very far from the protection of his own spear.

A Greek artist of about 500 BC does not dwell on Achilles' anxiety for his friend's well-being, but instead illustrates his practical response to this unfortunate turn of events (Fig. 23). Achilles, youthful and beardless, is shown squatting to the right. In his haste to succour his friend, he has not even removed his helmet but is intent upon his task of bandaging Patroklos' arm. Here we see the hero already putting to good use the lessons in medicine he had learned from Cheiron.

Patroklos is seated on a shield, none too comfortably. One foot is tucked in, while the other is braced against the border of the image – it fills the centre of a cup. He turns away from Achilles (perhaps to conceal the pain he is feeling) and grits his teeth. They are painted white and, although small, are conspicuous. He has taken off his helmet but still wears the cap that protected the head beneath it. Clearly both warriors have scarcely left the field of battle and yet the scene is an intensely quiet one, dominated by Achilles' concentration on his delicate task.

In the exact centre of the circular picture is Achilles' left hand, drawn with immense care, ever so gently adjusting the bandage around Patroklos' arm. Achilles' hands were 'man-slaying hands', so Homer tells us. Here they are very differently engaged. Patroklos elicited a very special quality of emotion from Achilles, perhaps the most powerful and tender feelings Achilles was capable of.

When he returned to the battle, Achilles continued to fight bravely and he was finally able to turn back the vigorous attack led by Telephos, the king of the Mysians. Telephos fled, thus preserving his life, but in his haste he tripped over a vine and so was not able to escape being wounded by Achilles.

23. Achilles bandages wounded Patroklos, Attic red-figure cup interior, about 500 BC, by the Sosias Painter, Berlin, Charlottenburg.

The discomfited Greeks eventually re-embarked and sailed for home, only to be caught and scattered in severely damaging storms.

*

After some time the allies reassembled at Argos. Not all were agreed that the enterprise should be resumed, especially since they realised the hopelessness of getting to Troy without the help of a well-informed guide. At this point Telephos arrived. The wound he had received from Achilles had never healed properly and when he consulted the oracle of Apollo on the subject, he was advised that the cure could only come from the agent that had inflicted the injury. He travelled to Argos, therefore, to ask for Achilles' help.

But Telephos, being recognised as a former enemy, was not kindly received. To save his life, he sought sanctuary at an altar. Such was the traditional tale; but when the early 5th century BC playwright Aeschylus took up the subject, in a tragedy now lost, he expanded it by introducing the idea that Agamemnon's wife, Klytaimnestra, took pity on the suppliant and placed the baby Orestes, Agamemnon's much treasured only son, in Telephos' arms. This, of course, gave additional force to Telephos' entreaty.

A contemporary Athenian vase painter, impressed by the piteous scene that Aeschylus had created, portrayed Telephos seated on the altar, a bandage round the festering wound in his thigh, holding in one hand the spear that identifies him as a warrior and with the other gently securing the little Orestes who hovers improbably above his lap (Fig. 24).

Art, life and myth were not strictly separated in ancient Greece, though it is not always entirely clear in which direction the influence flowed. Aeschylus was an admirer of the brilliant Athenian general Themistokles, who led the Greeks to victory over the Persians in the battle of Salamis in 480 BC, but who later fell out of favour with the Athenians. Themistokles was eventually forced to flee for his life. He fled from one place to another. The historian Thucydides reports:

> ... he was on one occasion so hard pressed that he had to rest at the house of Admetus, the King of the Molossi, who was no friend of his. Admetus happened not to be there at the time, and Themistokles was instructed by the king's wife, to whom he applied as a suppliant, to take their child in his arms and to sit down by the hearth. Before long Admetus returned and Themistokles told him who he was ... Admetus listened to him and then raised him to his feet, together with his own child, whom Themistokles had been holding in his arms as he sat there – and this indeed had had the greatest effect on the success of his supplication.
>
> Thucydides *History of the Peloponnesian War* I, 136.1-137.1 (trans. Warner)

The scene must have been very like that portrayed on the vase (Fig. 24). It is more likely that Aeschylus was trying to summon up before the eyes of his Athenian audience an image of the ill-treated Themistokles, than that Themistokles' life was following the pattern set down by the myth – though this possibility cannot be ruled out.

24. Telephos, holding the infant Orestes, seeks sanctuary on an altar, Attic red-figure pelike, about 450 BC, by a painter near the Chicago Painter, London, British Museum.

When Euripides took up the theme some time later in one of his tragedies (of which only traces now survive), he embellished the story further. He made Telephos cautiously approach the hostile Greeks in disguise; he came dressed as a beggar (rather a shocking innovation on

25. Telephos, seated on an altar, threatening the baby Orestes, Campanian red-figure hydria, about 330-310 BC, by the Ixion Painter, Naples, Museo Nazionale.

the stage at the time and one that made a great impression). When Telephos' true identity was discovered, he began to fear for his life. In panic he decided to use the infant Orestes as a hostage and threatened to kill the baby. This tense situation caught the imagination of a South Italian vase painter (Fig. 25). Telephos, his thigh bandaged because of the incurable wound, is shown kneeling on the altar dangling the helpless Orestes by one foot, his naked sword menacing Orestes' defenceless body. To the right are Orestes' distraught parents: Agamemnon with drawn sword, Klytaimnestra trying to restrain her husband from any precipitate action that might endanger the baby. To the left, and in the upper right corner (barely visible in the photograph) women express dismay.

Eventually everything came right. It was revealed that Telephos was actually a Greek – a chain of peculiar circumstances had led to his being king of the Mysians – and that he was willing to lead the Greeks to Troy, though reluctantly, since he had a Trojan wife. As Telephos embodied the guide who was so badly needed, Achilles was prevailed upon to cure the wound he had inflicted. This was not as simple as it seemed. Achilles' efforts were so ineffectual that some versions of the story say that he confessed he was quite ignorant of medicine. Once again it was the clever Odysseus who came to the rescue. He saw that it was not *Achilles* who had inflicted the wound, but rather his *spear*. On his advice some of the rust from the spear was scraped into Telephos' wound and that did the trick.

*

With renewed enthusiasm, the Greeks prepared once more to set out for Troy to recover Helen. They mustered at Aulis, and there they waited for a favourable wind. But to no avail. The troops grew restless, sullen, difficult to manage. The tragedian Aeschylus paints the scene:

> ... no ship sailed, no pail was full,
> and the Achaian* people sulked
> fast against the shore at Aulis
> facing Chalkis, where the tides ebb and
> surge:

* 'Achaian' was one of the terms used by Homer and later poets to refer to the Greeks attacking Troy.

and the winds blew from the Strymon,
bearing
sick idleness, ships tied fast and hunger,
distraction of the mind, carelessness
for hull and cable,
with time's length bent to double
measure
by delay crumbled the flower and pride
of Argos...

Aeschylus *Agamemnon* 186-198
(trans. Lattimore)

The seer Kalchas was finally consulted. His message was a terrible one: the goddess Artemis was angry; she could be appeased only by the sacrifice of Agamemnon's virgin daughter Iphigeneia. Agamemnon faced a cruel dilemma: was he to betray the great army he had collected to avenge the loss of Helen or was he to betray his own beloved daughter who was young, tender and utterly innocent? Either way he was doomed.

In the end, Agamemnon decided to put the common good before his own personal concerns. This meant that he was obliged to entice his trusting child to Aulis and then have her throat cut.

Iphigeneia was tempted to Aulis with the promise of marriage to Achilles. Once safely arrived, she was gagged – to prevent her uttering curses on those who were about to kill her – and carried to the altar to be slain like a sacrificial animal. Here is how Aeschylus described the scene in one of his tragedies:

Her prayers, her cries, her virgin youth,
Counted for nothing.
The warriors would have their war.
The ritual began:
Father, priest and king, he prayed the
prayers,
Commanded attendants to swing her up,
Like a goat, over the altar,
Face down,
A gag on her lovely lips
In case she spoke ill-omened words,
And cursed the royal house.
Gagged, bridled, silent,
Saffron dress slipping to the ground,
She cast piteous looks, arrows of grief,
At the ministers of sacrifice.
She knew them each by name.
Often, at rich banquets
In her father's halls, she had sung to
them
In a pure, virgin voice,
Love and Honour for her father
As he poured wine for the god.

Aeschylus *Agamemnon* 227-247
(trans. Raphael and McLeish)

Euripides, in his last play, treated the story of Iphigeneia at Aulis. For him, the human tragedy loomed uppermost. In his play, Agamemnon dithers over whether to summon his daughter to Aulis or not. Iphigeneia was his eldest and his favourite child. One tradition claims that Artemis' anger sprang from the fact that Agamemnon had promised to sacrifice to her the most beautiful creature born in his realm in the year of Iphigeneia's birth, but that he broke his vow when he saw Iphigeneia. The tie between father and daughter was a powerful and loving one.

When Iphigeneia arrived at Aulis, she rushed to greet her father, touchingly open and affectionate. His replies to her tender endearments were, not surprisingly, guarded and full of double meanings.

Iph: Father, I am so glad to see you. It has been so long.
Ag: And your father to see you. You speak for us both.
Iph: Greetings! Thank you, father, for bringing me to you.
Ag: Perhaps, my child, and perhaps not. I do not know.
Iph: Ah! How uneasy you look, for one who is glad to see me.
Ag: A king and general has much to think about.
Iph: Attend to me now. Forget your worries.
Ag: I am altogether with you now, my thoughts are nowhere else.
Iph: Then away with your frown, smooth your brow and make it friendly.

Ag: There! I am as happy as I can be to see you.
Iph: And yet the tears are pouring from your eyes?
Ag: The separation to come is long.
Iph: I do not understand what you say, dearest father, I do not understand.
Ag: Your sensible remarks move me the more to pity.
Iph: Then I will talk nonsense, if I can make you happy so.
Euripides *Iphigeneia at Aulis* 640-654
(trans. Hadas and McLean)

But eventually the horrible truth came out. Klytaimnestra, who, to Agamemnon's dismay, had accompanied her daughter to what she thought would be a wedding, finally confronted her husband with the ugly reality:

'... Three girls I bore you and a son, and now
You rob me of the first! Your reason, pray,
If men should ask it? O, I'll answer that, –
To win back Helen! Your own child for a wanton,
Your dearest for a foe! A proper bargain!
If you do this, if you are long at Troy,
What will my heart be like, think you, at home,
When I look at my daughter's empty chair,
And empty room, sitting there all alone,
Companied by my tears, still muttering,
"Your father killed you, child, killed you himself!" '
Euripides *Iphigeneia at Aulis* 1164-1178
(trans. Stawell)

Iphigeneia, appalled, frightened, then pleaded with her father for her life. Agamemnon was in anguish, but matters now had gone too far to be stopped. The troops had heard of Iphigeneia's arrival, and they demanded her death. There was no way out. Even Achilles' brave offer to defend the girl against all the odds was doomed to failure.

And then, suddenly, a new idea came to Iphigeneia:

'Mother, let me speak!
This anger with my father is in vain,
Vain to use force for what we cannot win.
Thank our brave friend for all his generous zeal,
But never let us broil him with the host,
No gain to us, and ruin for himself.
I have been thinking, mother, – hear me now! –
I have chosen death: it is my own free choice.
I have put cowardice away from me.
Honour is mine now. O, mother, say I am right!
Our country – think, our Hellas* – looks to me,
On me the fleet hangs now, the doom of Troy,
Our women's honour all the years to come.
My death will save them, and my name be blest,
She who freed Hellas! Life is not so sweet
I should be craven. You who bore your child,
It was for Greece you bore her, not yourself.
Think! Thousands of our soldiers stand to arms,
Ten thousand man the ships, and all on fire
To serve their outraged country, die for Greece:
And is my one poor life to hinder all? ...'
Euripides *Iphigeneia at Aulis* 1368-1390
(trans. Stawell)

Thus, according to Euripides, did Iphigeneia go willingly, even heroically, to her death.

Artemis, who demanded the maiden's sacrifice, at the last minute replaced Iphigeneia with a deer and carried the girl off to serve her at her sanctuary among the far-away Taurians. But Iphigeneia was never seen alive again by either of her parents.

Euripides' moving image of the blameless girl nobly prepared to sacrifice her life for what she believes is a higher cause must have inspired a South Italian vase painter, who showed Iphigeneia

* The Greeks' name for Greece.

26. Iphigenia willingly goes to her death, Apulian red-figure volute krater, 360-350 BC, by a painter related to the Iliupersis Painter, London, British Museum.

approaching the altar and the menacing knife with resigned determination (Fig. 26). Her ultimate salvation is hinted at by the deer which rears up behind her, almost shadowing her, and the presence of Artemis herself above and to the right. To the left, Apollo, holding a laurel branch, is seated watching the action, while a youthful acolyte and a woman assist.

The earlier tradition, namely that Iphigeneia was carried by main force to the altar and slaughtered like an animal, is reflected in an unattractive Roman wall painting (Fig. 27). The over-large figure of the priest and seer Kalchas stands to the right, while two men carry the histrionically gesturing Iphigeneia toward the stiff statue of Artemis standing on top of a column – the goddess herself appears in the sky to summon the substitute deer. There is little to move the heart in this insensitive picture – except for the veiled, mourning figure of Agamemnon, face covered, turning away from the action for which he is both chief agent and chief sufferer. This moving image was borrowed from a famous painting (now lost) by the 4th century BC artist Timanthes. The Roman writer Pliny, remarking on his ingenuity and inventiveness, cites in particular:

> … that *Iphigeneia*, praised by the orators, whom he depicted standing by the altar ready for death. Having represented all the onlookers and especially her father's brother as plunged in sorrow and having thus exhausted every presentiment of grief, he has veiled the face of her father, for which he had reserved no adequate expression.
>
> Pliny the Elder *Natural History* 35, 73 (trans. Jex-Blake)

Timanthes knew what he was about better than Pliny realised. By concealing

27. Iphigenia carried to be sacrificed, Roman wall painting, AD 63-79, Naples, Museo Nazionale.

the face of Agamemnon, Timanthes liberated us to imagine a grief more powerful than any that could be portrayed. The Roman painter, who has chosen to follow a different tradition from Timanthes in the matter of how Iphigeneia met her death and who had only limited ability when attempting to portray people's emotions, recognised the brilliance of Timanthes' invention, and applied it here – providing the one redeeming feature in his otherwise banal representation of one of the most truly horrifying episodes in the whole history of the Trojan war.

28. Ganymede, Attic red-figure bell krater, about 500-490 BC, by the Berlin Painter, Paris, Louvre.

3

Troy

So far we have been looking at the development of the conflict from the Greek point of view. Now we must take into account the Trojan background. For, by the time the Greeks under Agamemnon were preparing their assault on Troy, this proud city had already had a long and glorious history and had even suffered a devastating sack at the hands of some earlier Greeks led by the hero Herakles.

While the beauty of a woman, Helen, played a pivotal role on the Greek side of the legend, on the Trojan side it was the beauty of certain men that proved critical. Hekabe's suggestion that Helen had been dazzled by Paris' good looks (p. 24) was in tune with this tradition, for Troy could boast some of the handsomest males in myth. Many were so good-looking that even the gods could not resist them. Thus Zeus became enamoured of Ganymede, Eos, the dawn-goddess, of Tithonos, and even Aphrodite herself of Anchises, to whom she bore her son, Aeneas. The consequences to the city of these divine attachments were, of course, considerable.

*

Ganymede, according to Homer, was the most beautiful of mortals. He was one of three sons of Tros, an early king of Troy. Zeus, smitten by his beauty, carried him off to serve as cup-bearer among the gods and favoured him with the combined gifts of immortality and eternal youth. To compensate Tros for the loss of his son, Zeus gave the Trojan king some marvellous horses. These splendid, much-admired creatures later became the cause of Herakles' sack of the city, a generation before the trouble about Helen began.

Zeus' abduction of Ganymede became a popular subject with Athenian vase painters around the beginning of the 5th century BC. The vase painters enjoyed imagining the scene as a sort of amorous chase and represented it frequently for about half a century.

An elegant early image shows Ganymede alone on one side of a vase (Fig. 28), while Zeus, in dignified pursuit, appears on the other side (not illustrated). The ambivalence of the boy's flight is subtly, but unmistakably, hinted at: for although Ganymede appears to be fleeing his divine suitor, as decency requires, he is not actually running very fast. Furthermore no one at the time could miss the significance of the fact that the boy is represented conspicuously holding a cock in one hand. The cock was a traditional love-gift offered by homosexual suitors to the youthful objects of their affection in 5th century BC Athens. Ganymede moves to the right, but he turns his head to look back to the left; he holds the cock in his upturned left hand; with his down-turned right hand, he rolls a hoop. The geometric purity of the circular hoop – an attribute that suggests the boy's tender age – contrasts with the supple, living form of the youth. The careful opposition of one hand palm up with the other hand palm down, of the feet pointing to the right with the head turned to the left, produces a dynamic balance, both harmonious and full of vitality.

Ganymede is isolated on the large black surface of the vessel, but his extended arms and legs break up the space so that the lone figure is made to constitute an effective piece of decoration. The final triumph of the artist is the fact that he has made this meticulously contrived image appear perfectly natural.

Another vase painter shows Zeus, dignity thrown to the winds, in hot pursuit of his quarry, sceptre held in one outstretched hand, the other with fingers extended, ready to grasp the elusive boy (Fig. 29). Here Ganymede has put on more speed. He holds his hoop in front of him and dashes away from the eager god. In his haste, he unveils his enticing body. Does the vase painter mean to suggest that this is an accident or is he rather hinting that there might be something intentional, perhaps even provocative, in the gesture?

A third vase, from the middle of the century, shows Zeus having overtaken Ganymede: the two figures overlap within the tondo in the centre of a cup (Fig. 30). As Zeus braces his feet against the rim of the circle, he drops his sceptre and lets fall his thunderbolt (to the left). Ganymede holds the bird in one hand, while the fingers of the other are spread wide in protest. Diagonals cross or complement each other: Ganymede's right thigh meets Zeus' at an angle, but his lower left leg is parallel to Zeus' lower right leg; the two figures lean away from one another, yet look toward each other; the centrifugal impulse of their bodies pulling apart is returned to the centre by the heads turned inwards; limbs criss-cross but the lucid drawing clearly disentangles the overlapping bodies. The tension of the encounter, the urgency of the god, the confusion of the boy are all condensed, compressed within the round frame, the figures dynamically interlocked and yet brilliantly balanced in movement and counter-movement within the circle.

After the middle of the 5th century BC this kind of encounter fell out of favour with artists and from the 4th century BC the rape of Ganymede came to be represented in quite another way. We hear of a famous image (now lost) by the

30. Zeus and Ganymede, Attic red-figure cup interior, about 455 BC, by the Penthesilea Painter, Ferrara, Museo Archeologico di Spina.

Fig 39

29. Zeus and Ganymede, Attic red-figure kantharos, about 490-480 BC, by the Brygos Painter, Boston, Museum of Fine Arts (Perkins Collection).

Fig. 38

sculptor Leochares which illustrates the new fashion: it portrayed

> an eagle carrying off Ganymede in which the bird is aware of what his burden is and for whom he is carrying it, and is careful not to let his claws hurt the boy even through his clothes ...
>
> Pliny the Elder *Natural History* 34,79 (trans. Rackham)

This type was not only reproduced in sculpture but became popular in Roman mosaics as well (Fig. 31). Ganymede is now very clearly characterised as a *Trojan* youth (one might have mistaken him for an Athenian in the vase paintings). He wears a soft, peaked hat that flops over at the top, known as a 'Phrygian cap' which is used to identify Trojans like Ganymede or Paris.

Ganymede's task, once abducted, was to act as cup-bearer for the gods. A late 6th century BC Athenian vase shows him performing this duty, serving wine to Zeus himself (Fig. 32). Ganymede stands at the centre of the painted exterior of a cup, attentively facing his master. Zeus holds his thunderbolt in one hand and extends a libation bowl in the other, as Ganymede prepares to pour some wine from a jug. Hestia, goddess of the hearth, grasping a bunch of flowers, sits opposite Zeus. Behind her sits lovely Aphrodite, wearing a smart turban, holding a bird in one hand and a flower in the other, turning round to speak to the war god, Ares. Athena, having doffed her helmet for this informal occasion, is seated behind Zeus and turns to talk to Hermes. It is, altogether, a most illustrious

31. Ganymede carried off by the eagle, Roman mosaic, late Imperial period, Sousse, Museum (Tunisia).

32. Ganymede serving wine to Zeus amid an assembly of the gods, Attic red-figure cup exterior, late 6th century BC, by Oltos, Tarquinia, Museo Nazionale.

33. Ganymede serving the eagle, Roman sarcophagus relief, end of the 2nd century AD, Vatican, Cortile del Belvedere.

assemblage, and Ganymede has earned an honourable place within it.

On a Roman relief (Fig. 33), by contrast, Ganymede offers a drink not to Zeus but to an eagle. Notice the Phrygian cap. A personification, difficult to identify precisely, lies beneath the eagle. Zeus is nowhere to be seen, unless the eagle, instead of being his messenger or attribute, is meant to be the god himself in disguise. Lucian addresses this problematic ambiguity in his usual humorous manner in the following dialogue:

> ZEUS: All right, Ganymede, now that I've got you here, you can give me a kiss – just to make sure that the hooked beak and sharp claws have really gone.
>
> GANYMEDE: [*turning round and staring*] Why, you're a human being! But weren't you an eagle a moment ago? Didn't you come swooping down and whisk me away from my sheep? What's happened to all your feathers? Are you moulting, or what? You look completely different all of a sudden.
>
> ZEUS: No, my boy, I'm not really an eagle. Nor am I a human being. [*Grandly.*] You see before you the king of all the gods. [*Reverting to an ordinary tone.*] That eagle business was just a temporary disguise. ...
>
> Lucian *Dialogues of the Gods* 10, 209 (trans. Turner)

Being the love-object of a god was seldom an entirely happy experience. Ganymede did unusually well. Another Trojan prince, Tithonos, some two generations younger than Ganymede, was not quite so lucky. He, too, caught the eye of a divinity, in this case the amorous goddess of the dawn, Eos, who, despite her unsociable working hours, was always hungry for lovers. She eagerly brought Tithonos to her bed and in the ecstasy of her emotion asked that he should be made immortal. Her wish was granted, but it turned out badly for Tithonos, for she had forgotten to ask for him also to retain eternal youth (like Ganymede). The result was that the poor man grew older and frailer as time went on, but could never claim the escape of death. His immortality became a curse rather than a blessing.

Artists were not eager to represent the terrible and relentless old age of Tithonos, but chose rather to show him in the flower of his youth, the way he looked when he first appeared as an object of desire to Eos. They often portrayed the youth fleeing from the goddess in very much the same schema as they used when showing Ganymede fleeing from Zeus. Fig. 34 is a typical example. Tithonos carries a lyre – this distinguishes him from other amorous attachments of Eos. Eos herself is usually, but not always, shown winged; thus she can float down, as here, or

34. Eos pursuing Tithonos, Attic red-figure pelike, 460-450 BC, by the Niobid Painter, London, British Museum.

36. Eos carrying off Tithonos, Attic red-figure skyphos, about 450-440 BC, by the Lewis Painter, Cambridge, Fitzwilliam Museum.

35. Eos and Tithonos, Attic red-figure cup interior, about 470 BC, by the Telephos Painter, Boston, Museum of Fine Arts (Perkins Collection).

simply run along the ground, as elsewhere (Figs. 35 and 36). Tithonos is often represented trying to escape from the aggressive goddess; but sometimes he is portrayed already in her clutches (Fig. 35). Eos, here, braces her feet against the edge of the circular border in the centre of a cup very much as Zeus does in Fig. 30, and Tithonos tries to flee, just as Ganymede does. But although the emotional situations are similar and the shape to be filled is the same, it is easy to see that the quality of the artists is very different. The vase painter of Fig. 30 filled his circle with an exciting and dynamic pattern; the one who decorated Fig. 35 has left great uneven gaps around and especially above his figures. Eos' wings occupy a lot of space, but she and Tithonos are small and ungainly. The goddess is as importunate as the god, the youth as reluctant as Ganymede, but all drama has gone out of the scene. Tithonos is unattractively skinny; Eos, with her upturned head and heavenward-gaze, is absurdly sentimental; the composition is weak, and even the firm drawing cannot redeem this mediocre work.

Sometimes painters rendered Eos actually carrying off the object of her desire (Fig. 36). In this example Eos is not winged, but she is recognisable still, for no other goddess is so assertive in her pursuit of a lover, and no Greek woman could ever be imagined so. The youth in her arms grasps a lyre. This identifies him as Tithonos. There is no hint of the unhappy end of the story, but the way Eos holds Tithonos as if he were an overgrown child might be intended to recall to the viewer the son that Eos was to bear him, the gallant Memnon who was destined to die fighting on behalf of his father's city (p. 92).

The third Trojan prince to captivate a divine lover was Anchises. Aphrodite seduced him while he was playing the lyre and tending his herds on Mount Ida. She pretended that she was just a mortal woman but used her divine power to arouse an overwhelming passion in him. After she had her way with him, she revealed her true and rather frightening identity. A *Homeric Hymn to Aphrodite* tells the story at length. In conclusion Aphrodite recalls the other Trojan princes whose beauty drew the gods to them as lovers, Ganymede and Tithonos. She says:

> 'So also golden-throned Eos rapt away Tithonos who was of your race and like the deathless gods. And she went to ask the dark-clouded Son of Kronos* that he should be deathless and live eternally and Zeus bowed his head to her prayer and fulfilled her desire. Too simple was queenly Eos: she thought not in her heart to ask youth for him and to strip him of the slough of deathly age. So while he enjoyed the sweet flower of life he lived rapturously with golden-throned Eos, the early-born, by the streams of Ocean, at the ends of the earth; but when the first grey hairs began to ripple from his comely head and noble chin, queenly Eos kept away from his bed, though she cherished him in her house and nourished him with food and ambrosia and gave him rich clothing. But when loathsome old age pressed full upon him, and he could not move or lift his limbs, this seemed to her in her heart the best counsel: she laid him in a room and put to the shining doors. There he babbles endlessly, and no more has strength at all, such as once he had in his supple limbs.
>
> I would not have you be deathless among the deathless gods and live continually after such sort ...'
>
> *Hymn to Aphrodite* 5, 218-240
> (trans. Evelyn-White)

Thus Aphrodite assured Anchises that he would be spared a cruel immortality and an interminable old age. She then went on to tell him of the son she would bear him and who would be a great joy to him.

This boy was Aeneas, and he indeed proved to be a wonderful comfort to his father. The filial piety of Aeneas was so celebrated and so touching that when artists thought of Anchises, they thought more about his relationship to his son than about his attachment to the divine Aphrodite. Hardly any representations of Anchises with Aphrodite survive from antiquity, but there are, by contrast, very many that show Anchises with Aeneas. Most of these are in the context of illustrations of the fall of Troy, for in a time of crisis the depth of Aeneas' loyalty to his father was most fully revealed.

The Roman poet Virgil painted a haunting picture of the horrors that befell Troy on the night it was sacked. He described the brutal murders and the savage destruction of the city in powerfully evocative verses. He had Aeneas recount how, as the blood flowed and the flames rose all around, he resolved to rescue his aged father, advising the frail old man:

> 'Come now, you must let them lift you onto my back. I will hold my shoulders ready for you. This labour of love will be no weight for me.'
>
> Virgil *Aeneid* 2, 707-708
> (trans. Jackson Knight)

By the time of Virgil in the late 1st century BC, the tradition that Aeneas had

* Zeus.

37. Aeneas carrying Anchises, fleeing Troy under the guidance of Aphrodite, oinochoe, Attic black-figure on a white ground, about 510-500 BC, by the Painter of Louvre F 118, Paris, Louvre.

saved his father by carrying him bodily out of the ravaged city was already an old one. It was depicted on numerous black-figure vases during the 6th century BC (Fig. 37). Aeneas was shown armed, wearing a helmet and carrying a shield in one hand and a pair of spears in the other. Anchises, perched on his son's shoulders, clings to his back. Aeneas, despite the fact that he holds the spears in his right hand, folds his arm protectively around the tucked-up knees of his father. Aphrodite often appears in this scene. She was, after all, like Thetis, the divine mother of a mortal son and like any mother she was always concerned for the welfare of her child. The vase painters who portrayed Aphrodite showed her standing behind Aeneas, one hand raised to encourage him on his way and to ensure, by her divine protection, his successful escape from the fallen city. Did they imagine that while she watched over her son, Aphrodite also might have given some thought to his father, the withered old man who had once been so beautiful and had captivated her heart long years before on Mount Ida?

*

Laomedon, the uncle of Anchises and father of Tithonos, was for a time the king of Troy. While he was king, the gods Poseidon and Apollo contracted to work for him for a year. According to one tradition, Poseidon built the walls of Troy, while Apollo tended the flocks; according to another, both gods worked on the walls, employing a mortal to help with one part. His section, naturally, was weaker than the rest.

When the time came for Laomedon to give his divine servants the payment he had promised them, he just laughed at their simplicity and sent them away with threats. But gods could not be dismissed so easily, nor did they take broken promises lightly.

The offended deities set about punishing the impious king and his people. Apollo sent a plague and Poseidon a sea monster. There was great distress throughout the city. Laomedon was informed that there

38. Herakles and Hesione fight the sea-monster, Corinthian black-figure krater, about 570-560 BC, Boston, Museum of Fine Arts (Helen and Alice Colburn Fund).

was only one way out of these grave afflictions: he must sacrifice his lovely daughter Hesione to the sea monster. Slippery though he was, Laomedon was soon forced to see that he had no choice in the matter.

The maiden was exposed in a prominent position and the threat from the sea monster was imminent when the hero Herakles happened to pass by. He offered to save the girl in exchange for the wonderful horses that had been given to Tros in recompense for Ganymede. Laomedon agreed. Herakles set to work briskly.

Fig. 38 is an early 6th century BC Corinthian representation of Herakles and Hesione confronting the toothy monster. Herakles has already shot off four arrows and is about to let fly the fifth. Hesione has not stood idly by but has come to the aid of her saviour by throwing stones. The monster, who has been hit in the chin by one arrow and is beaten about the face with stones, looks as if it is on the brink of expiring.

Herakles, having saved the girl, was now in a position to claim his reward. He was not, however, free to take the horses with him right away. He therefore told Laomedon to keep them for him until he was able to fetch them.

Some time later Herakles returned to Troy to pick up the horses. But Laomedon, who thought he had been clever in cheating the gods, now thought he might be clever in cheating a hero. He refused to hand the horses over. Herakles departed in anger and proceeded to gather an army to punish the city of the perfidious king. He was joined by many illustrious heroes, among them Telamon and the young Philoktetes, and in six ships (according to Homer) or 18 (according to others) set off to attack Troy and to win by force what he had earned through kindness.

Along the way Herakles stopped off at the sanctuary of Chryse in order to sacrifice to the local goddess. Fig. 39 illustrates the scene. Herakles, bearded and wearing a wreath on his head, stands slightly to the left of centre, beckoning to the youth in charge of the sacrificial animal. To the right is a rough stone altar with a fire burning on it, behind which the stiff statue of the goddess stands on a column. Further right a winged female figure assists. She is the goddess of victory and her presence bodes well for the expedition. A second boy helps at the far right. A fragmentary vase (Fig. 40) shows a later stage in the sacrifice, when the victim has already been slain and meat is being roasted over the altar fire. Only the lower part of the statue of the

39. Herakles sacrifices to Chryse, with Nike (victory) assisting, Attic red-figure bell krater, about 410-400 BC, by an imitator of the Kadmos Painter, Vienna, Kunsthistorisches Museum.

40. Herakles sacrifices to Chryse assisted by Philoktetes and another youth, fragments of an Attic red-figure bell krater, about 430 BC, by the Painter of London E 494, London, British Museum.

goddess is preserved here, placed on a column between the rough stone altar and the boy to the right. Another boy stood between Herakles and the altar and though most of his figure is lost, part of his name is preserved. He was Philoktetes and this sacrifice to Chryse was to loom large in his later life (pp. 54–5).

The sacrifice completed, Herakles and his heroic band continued their journey to Troy.

This military assault on Laomedon's city was portrayed on one of the pediments that decorated a temple on the island of Aigina in the early years of the 5th century BC (Fig. 41). Artists, who at this time were seeking to make their images as naturalistic as possible, had recently found a solution to the awkward problem of filling the long low triangle of a pediment with a unified subject, peopled by figures depicted on a single scale. They did this by depicting a scene of violence and placing a deity in the centre of the conflict. The deity, in this case the goddess Athena, would naturally be supposed to be larger than the surrounding mortals and so was useful for filling the apex of the triangle. The combatants on either side could be shown on a uniform scale and still contained within the pediment because some of them stood, others crouched and still others lay upon the ground. The heights of their heads were thus conveniently adjusted to the slope of the pediment and their poses could be rationally explained as consequences of the fight they were engaged in.

Just which battle is represented at Aigina would be difficult to determine were it not for the archer kneeling to the right (Fig. 42). He does not wear an ordinary helmet like most of the others but is wearing the head of a skinned lion over his own head instead. Only one hero is attired in this way: Herakles.

The skin came from the Nemean lion, a ferocious beast that Herakles had been required to kill as the first of his many labours. This labour was particularly difficult because the lion was invulnerable and so its hide could not be penetrated by any weapon. Herakles eventually had to strangle it with his bare hands. He used the lion's own claws (which could cut through *anything*) to flay the beast and often was portrayed by artists wearing its pelt as a kind of primitive cloak (Figs. 46 and 79). In Fig. 42 he is shown using the

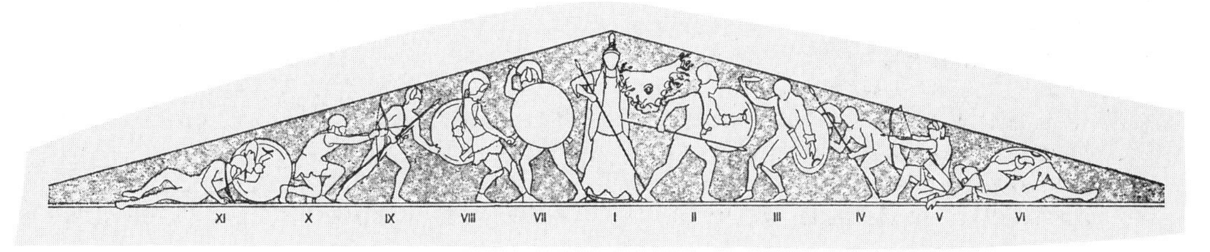

41. The First Greek War against Troy led by Herakles, reconstruction drawing of the East Pediment of the temple of Aphaia at Aigina by D. Ohly, early 5th century BC.

head in place of a helmet, his face framed within its jaws.

Herakles was a celebrated archer, who was equipped with poisoned arrows that made his every shot deadly. He is here depicted drawing his bow. His kneeling posture has suited him for a position near one corner of the pediment in what might seem a surprisingly inconspicuous location for the leader of the expedition. Pride of place near the centre must have been reserved for his comrade Telamon, who was a local hero in Aigina. (Telamon's son Ajax was also a local hero and probably figured prominently in the pediment at the other end of the temple, which featured the second, later sack of Troy, the one accomplished by Agamemnon and his army.)

Troy quickly fell to the Greek onslaught led by Herakles. Laomedon was punished, the city was sacked and the spoils were distributed among the victors. The princess Hesione, no longer a princess in her devastated land, was given as a prize to Herakles' comrade Telamon. But Herakles felt that he still had a special relationship with Hesione and so he allowed her the privilege of ransoming one of her fellow captives and saving him from execution or slavery. She chose her brother Priam, who now became the new king of Troy.

*

Once Trojan perfidy had been requited, Herakles departed. But for Troy the matter did not end so simply, for the city was destined to fall not once but twice under the attack of Herakles' powerful bow. The second time the weapon was no longer wielded by the mighty hero himself, but by his young companion Philoktetes, now grown to manhood.

The bow passed to Philoktetes when Herakles was dying – or rather, when he *wished* to die and Philoktetes alone was willing to help him accomplish this end. The peculiar circumstances which

42. Herakles as an archer fighting against Laomedon's Troy, from the East Pediment of the temple of Aphaia at Aigina, Munich, Glyptothek.

brought the hero to such an extraordinary pass arose from the scheming of a lecherous centaur, Nessos, and the unwitting complicity of Herakles' jealous wife, Deianeira.

Nessos met Deianeira when Herakles and Deianeira, early in their married life, had to cross a river. Herakles had no problem swimming to the other side, but his delicate bride was grateful to accept the services of Nessos, who was the local ferryman. As Nessos was a centaur, he was well fitted by his physique for his profession. He did his ferrying efficiently by setting his passengers on his back.

Nessos was a very different sort of centaur from the wise Cheiron. Although Cheiron and Nessos were both part man and part horse, in Cheiron civilised human attitudes predominated, while in Nessos primitive animal instincts prevailed. These prompted Nessos to take an all-too-personal interest in his pretty passenger.

An Athenian vase painter in the late 6th century BC (Fig. 43) fitted the story neatly into the round centre of the interior of a cup. He portrayed Deianeira seated somewhat anxiously on the cen-

43. Nessos carrying Herakles' wife Deianeira, Attic red-figure cup interior, about 520 BC, by the Ambrosios Painter, London, British Museum.

taur's back. The names of the protagonists written near the edge of the border not only serve to identify them but also to fill vacant bits of space and emphasise the circular shape. Nessos' tail and his hind legs – before the cup was broken and this portion lost – completed the decoration of the lower part.

As he gallops along, Nessos turns and puts his arms around the girl. Perhaps he is trying to steady her. The scene is one of remarkable tenderness, and while there may be some suggestion that the centaur is about to steal a kiss, there is no hint that he has a violent rape in mind. Deianeira's stiff hands with their rigidly extended fingers conform to the artistic conventions of the time and yet, within this context, they seem to suggest that she is tense and ill at ease – quite rightly so as it turned out, for one thing inevitably led to another and soon the outraged Deianeira had to cry out to Herakles for help.

When Deianeira raised the alarm, Herakles could only respond to her promptly by shooting Nessos with one of his poisoned arrows. As Nessos expired he advised Deianeira to collect some of his blood and to preserve it carefully to use as a love-charm should Herakles ever fail in his devotion to her. He assured Deianeira that if she were to rub this blood into a garment for Herakles, once Herakles had put it on, he would never love another woman. Deianeira took his advice.

Vase painters with only a limited space available for decoration seldom showed Herakles shooting at Nessos from a distance but drew instead a compact group (Fig. 44). At such close quarters a bow would have seemed to be an impractical weapon, and so the vase painters armed Herakles with a sword or a club. The compression of the image therefore subtly altered – or simply ignored – the content of the story.

In Fig. 44 the brisk, well-groomed hero is portrayed smartly dispatching the unfortunate centaur. Nessos is already collapsing at the knees under the powerful attack of Herakles. He extends his two hands in a dance-like gesture, touching Herakles' chin with one of them in order to supplicate for mercy. The image is given immediacy and impact by showing the two adversaries locked in combat; Herakles having overtaken Nessos and sprung on his back, grasps him by the hair and is about to thrust home his

44. Herakles killing Nessos, Attic black-figure amphora (neck), late 7th century BC, by the Nettos Painter, Athens, National Archaeological Museum.

45. Apotheosis of Herakles, Attic red-figure calyx krater, late 5th century BC, New York, Metropolitan Museum (Joseph Pulitzer Bequest).

sword. The artist may have assumed that the transaction between Nessos and Deianeira had already taken place or he may just not have been concerned with that aspect of the story.

The importance of Nessos' advice to Deianeira could not, however, be neglected when it came to the matter of Herakles' end. For a long time Deianeira felt no need to make use of Nessos' purported love-charm, but after some years she learned that Herakles had fallen in love with a younger woman. Anxious to regain his affection for herself, she sent Herakles a robe which she had rubbed with some of Nessos' blood. The result was disastrous. The poison from Herakles' arrow had seeped into the blood; it now began to eat away at Herakles' flesh. The hero's sufferings soon became unbearable. Indeed, he never loved another woman! But this was small consolation to Deianeira when Herakles cursed her for destroying him and declared that his only wish now was to die.

In intense agony, Herakles was finally put upon a pyre, but none of his attendants dared to set it alight. At last Herakles prevailed upon Philoktetes, who as a boy had accompanied him to Troy and assisted at his sacrifice to Chryse, to do him this service. As a reward Herakles gave Philoktetes his glorious bow and unerring arrows. It was these weapons that were destined to bring Troy down for a second time.

Death not only provided Herakles with release from his sufferings; it also opened the way to his apotheosis. The fire on the pyre supposedly burned away all that was mortal in Herakles, while the immortal part of him ascended to Olympus to dwell in everlasting bliss with the gods.

Herakles' apotheosis is the subject of a 5th century BC vase (Fig. 45). In the centre Herakles is shown, the club which

46. Comic version of the apotheosis of Herakles, Attic red-figure oinochoe, about 410-400 BC, by the Nikias Painter, Paris, Louvre.

was so often his weapon over his shoulder, standing in a chariot driven by a winged figure of victory. The chariot is shown the way by the messenger god, Hermes, while below, nymphs extinguish the pyre under the supervision of the helmeted goddess Athena. Notice in the top right corner a damaged figure of a man holding a bow and quiver; he must be Philoktetes.

Dignity, reverence and respect are laudable attitudes, and despite much energetic movement they characterise the scene represented in Fig. 45. But what is unexpectedly appealing about the ancient Greeks is not so much the praiseworthy seriousness of their treatment of mythology as their light-hearted ability to make fun of it. Thus on a slightly later vase (Fig. 46) we can see a parody of Herakles' apotheosis. The figure of victory who serves as charioteer is a snub-nosed urchin; Herakles himself is a tough-looking ruffian, and the chariot is drawn not by docile horses but by grumpy centaurs with their hands tied behind their backs in order to force them to perform this demeaning equine task.

Thus we see that even if Herakles, hero of many labours and conqueror of Troy, might transcend his terrible end, he still could not escape the biting wit of Greek artists.

4

The Greeks Go to Troy

By the time the Greeks under the leadership of Agamemnon were ready to set out for Troy for a second time (p. 34), they were beginning to appreciate what a difficult undertaking the war might turn out to be. They had already made a false start which took them to Mysia, but now that they had Telephos on their side as a guide, they were more confident that they would at least be able to find Troy. Beyond that, the omens were not good. While the troops were still mustered at Aulis, they had seen a serpent dart out from behind an altar and slither up into a nearby plane-tree. It devoured eight baby sparrows in a nest and finally also swallowed the mother-bird as she fluttered about wildly. It was then turned to stone. The prophet Kalchas explained to the startled troops that this was a sign that nine years would be consumed (like the sparrows) in the siege and that Troy would only be taken in the tenth year.

Anios, the king of Delos, was also aware of this dire prophecy. When the expedition arrived at Delos mid-way across the Aegean sea, he ingeniously suggested that the troops stay with him for the nine years' waiting time. He could afford to keep the army because of the marvellous gifts of his three daughters who were able to produce grain, olives and wine at will. At the time his offer was declined, but later, when the troops at Troy found themselves constantly forced to make foraging expeditions while trying to maintain the siege of Troy, they thought again. Anios' daughters seemed a general's dream commissariat and the Greeks decided to send one of the kings who shared the command of the army to demand their services. But by now the girls had become frightened of life with the troops and they fled. When relentlessly pursued, they prayed to the god Dionysos, who had bestowed such special gifts on them, and in the nick of time he transformed them into doves and they escaped.

The story of the daughters of Anios was so seldom illustrated in antiquity that when a South Italian vase turned up in the 1980s showing, among other things, three figures on an altar, scholars were at first baffled as to what it might represent (Fig. 47). The three figures consisted of a man, in the centre, sitting on the altar between a seated woman holding sheaves of grain and a standing woman holding a vine rich with grape clusters. The numerous subsidiary figures did not at first seem to offer any helpful clues. To the left of the central group stood a woman holding some leafy twigs, to the right a dignified man with a sceptre. Higher up, three divinities were represented: to the left, the goddess Artemis, identifiable by her attributes of bow and arrow, addressing her twin brother Apollo, seated with his attribute of a swan; to the right, a seated figure of Pan identifiable by his little white goat-horns. No inscriptions gave any hints about the identity of the other, more generic figures.

47. The Daughters of Anios, Apulian red-figure calyx krater, about 330 BC, by the Darius Painter, private collection, Miami, Florida.

Many such complex scenes with men and women holding rather ordinary objects seem to defy interpretation. Sometimes, luckily, as in this case, somebody who sees the 'mystery picture' recalls a story that might be related. If it fits the image, the secret may be unlocked.

Thus, once someone suggested that the vase (Fig. 47) might refer to the daughters of Anios, most of the elements suddenly arranged themselves into a more intelligible order. What had at first seemed to be a central scene of three figures on an altar flanked by a standing woman to the left and a standing man to the right now took on a somewhat different configuration. The rather inconspicuous woman to the left ceased to look as if she were just the symmetrical pendant to the standing man and began to look like one of three sisters, attaching herself, psychologically, to the other two with their more immediately eye-catching crops. At the same time, the leafy twigs she held began to look like sprigs of olive. The regal man standing at the right, instead of reflecting the stance of the olive-maiden, now began to look as if he were confronting the group of four, and the position of his right hand, which at first seemed so similar to that of the olive-maiden's left hand, now became a gesture suggesting that he was addressing the four figures.

Once the story had been identified, the image became clear: it was a representation of one of the Greek kings coming to Delos to request the services of Anios' daughters. Anios and his offspring, now reluctant to become involved in the expedition, have taken refuge on or beside an altar. The scene is set at Delos, an island sacred to Apollo, and so the appearance of the god and his sister Artemis (who were born there) seems appropriate. The reason for the presence of Pan is less obvious. It may be that he is there to indicate no more than that the events are taking place out of doors. We cannot always understand every detail that appears in ancient representations.

It has become apparent that the reading of a picture can be radically altered by the interpretation that is imposed on it, and even the composition can take on quite another structure once one knows what the story is about. This is quite natural and correct. Images on their own are mute. If they are intended to illustrate a story and the right story is identified, the elements will fall into place in accordance with the narrative, as here. The only dangers for the modern student are either that a story is *invented* to account for a picture, which would then have nothing to do with the original intentions of the artist, or that the wrong story is settled on and the elements are *forced* to conform with it.

Artists can sometimes insure against errors of interpretation by labelling their figures or choosing situations that are quite unmistakable. Often, however,

48. Philoktetes bitten by the snake, Attic red-figure stamnos, about 450 BC, by Hermonax, Paris, Louvre.

artists are simply straightforwardly illustrating a well-known story; but we, for whom the story is no longer such a familiar one, are left mystified.

*

The Greeks were anxious, once they were on their way to Troy again, to make sure that they did everything correctly. They therefore asked Philoktetes to guide them to the sanctuary of Chryse, where Herakles had made a sacrifice before his successful expedition against Troy. Philoktetes agreed with a willingness that he was later bitterly to regret.

While the Greeks were making their sacrifice, a snake emerged from somewhere near the altar and bit Philoktetes on the foot. The Athenian vase painter of Fig. 48 shows the rigid old-fashioned statue of Chryse, which we have already seen in Figs. 39 and 40, with the offending snake retreating to take cover by the base. Agamemnon is about to strike the snake with his staff, but the damage has already been done. Philoktetes lies on the ground to the right, his face distorted with pain, one arm thrown over his head in anguish. Three more Greeks look toward the snake with dismay and alarm, while a fourth has the presence of mind to try to comfort Philoktetes. But it was all to no avail.

The wound worsened and no remedy could be found. Philoktetes' agony became such that he could not contain his cries and the ill-omened sounds prevented any sacrifices being conducted properly. Furthermore the wound festered and stank. Philoktetes' presence became insupportable. It looked as if the whole expedition would be wrecked rather than furthered by the stop-over at Chryse's sanctuary. Something had to be done. The two generals, Agamemnon and Menelaos, in consultation with the clever Odysseus, therefore decided that Philoktetes should be set ashore on the island of Lemnos and that the bow and arrows of Herakles should be left with him so that he could shoot enough game to keep himself alive. It seemed a cruel decision, but an inevitable one.

To Philoktetes only the cruel side seemed self-evident. Sophokles, in his tragedy *Philoktetes*, painted a grim picture of what the hero's life was like. In the play, Philoktetes, after years of having been marooned on Lemnos, describes his situation to a visiting youth in the following words:

'... Those two generals
and Prince Odysseus of the
  Cephallenians
cast me ashore here to their shame, as
  lonely
as you can see me now, wasting with my
  sickness
as cruel as it is, caused by the murderous
  bite
of a viper mortally dangerous.
I was already bitten when we put in here
on my way from sea-encircled Chryse.
I tell you, boy, those men cast me away
  here
and ran and left me helpless. They were
  happy
when they saw that I had fallen asleep
  on the shore
in a rocky cave, after a rough passage.
They went away and left me with such
  rags –
and few enough of them – as one might
  give
an unfortunate beggar and a handful of
  food.
May god give them like!
Think, boy, of that awakening when I
  awoke
and found them gone; think of the
  useless tears
and curses on myself when I saw the
  ships –
my ships, which I had once commanded
  – gone,
all gone, and not a man left on the
  island,
not one to help me or to lend a hand
when I was seized with my sickness, not
  a man!
In all I saw before me nothing but pain;
but of that a great abundance, boy.'

Sophokles *Philoktetes* 264-284
(trans. Grene)

Philoktetes had to endure many years of such suffering before the Greeks thought of him again.

*

Once the Greeks landed at Troy, the fighting was often fierce, but it was not always a matter of mature warriors confronting one another in heroic combat. For instance, when Achilles learned of the prophecy that Troy could not fall if Priam's young son Troilos were to reach the age of twenty, he resolved to kill the boy and thus to eradicate this impediment.

The story of Troilos was probably told at some length in the *Kypria*, one of several epic poems composed not long after the time of Homer, which filled in parts of the traditional myths of the Trojan war that were not covered by Homer's poems, the *Iliad* and the *Odyssey*. The *Iliad* only described a few weeks when the Greeks were already in the tenth year of the war, while the *Odyssey* was devoted to a selection of events that took place after the fall of Troy. The *Kypria*, by contrast, dealt extensively with the circumstances leading up to the war and the early years of the fighting (discussed in our Chapters 1 and 2) and included an account of Troilos' death. Most of the poem is now lost, and we know about it only through later summaries and a few fragments that were preserved by chance, but the stories it recounted – if not the epic itself – must have been freely available to the vase painters of the 6th and 5th centuries BC.

While under siege, Troy was short of water and Troilos, a horse-loving boy, was obliged to venture outside the protective walls of the city in order to reach the fountain-house and water his horses. There Achilles hid to await him.

On Fig. 49 a column economically represents the fountain-house, and Achilles, armed with shield, helmet and spear, crouches behind it ready to ambush the youth. Polyxena, Troilos' sister, stands quietly on the other side of the column. She has come to the fountain-house to fetch water. Her water-jar is placed on the ground beneath a lion's-head spout, from which water gushes. Achilles, watchful in his hiding place, could not fail to notice the lovely girl. This glimpse Achilles caught of Polyxena was later to prove fatal for her,

49. Achilles prepares to ambush Troilos, Attic black-figure hydria shoulder, about 525-500 BC, by one of the painters of the Leagros Group, London, British Museum.

and according to some authorities, even for Achilles himself.

But the main focus of Achilles' attention now was Troilos, not Polyxena. Troilos is just behind Polyxena, riding one horse and leading another. He is followed by a youth carrying two spears, who cannot be identified with any certainty and was probably introduced by the vase-painter merely to fill up the space. The myth is depicted on the shoulder of a hydria (a water jar) very like the one Polyxena has placed under the spout. The field is a rather long, narrow one, the extent of which often seems to have proved something of an embarrassment to painters who had to introduce 'extras' into the story in order to fill out the composition.

Some vase painters liked to show Achilles lurking behind the fountain-house preparing to ambush Troilos; others preferred to show a later moment in the story when Achilles had already leapt out of his hiding place to attack the terrified boy. Fig. 50, which like Fig. 49 decorates the shoulder of a hydria, shows Achilles in fierce pursuit of Troilos. Troilos urges on his mount with desperate intensity and the riderless horse keeps pace with it. On either side of the central group, girls flee away. Archers wearing the peaked hats which identify them as Trojans frame the scene.

This vase is a good example of the balance that vase painters had to try to maintain between illustrating a story and decorating a vessel. In this case considerations of design seem to have weighed more heavily. The two fleeing girls, centrifugally symmetrical, are very effective as a compositional frame for the central group of Troilos and Achilles. But one of the girls, the one on the right, is more than just a piece of decoration. She is Polyxena, and in her fright she has dropped her water jar; it lies broken on the ground, conveniently filling the space

50. Achilles pursues Troilos, Attic black-figure hydria shoulder, about 520-510 BC, by the Antimenes Painter or his circle, Munich, Museum Antiker Kleinkunst.

51. Achilles pursues Troilos, Attic black-figure krater (François vase), about 570 BC, by Kleitias, Florence, Museo Archeologico.

beneath the bodies of the galloping horses.

Achilles, Troilos and Polyxena are the only characters who are essential for the story; the other figures are there just to make the picture look more balanced and to fill any unsightly gaps, but in doing so they actually compromise the clarity of the narrative.

Vase painters of greater talent were able both to create a beautiful piece of decoration and to tell a story in a meaningful way. Kleitias, whose name we know from his signature on some of the vases he painted, had such talent. In Fig. 51 he fills a long narrow frieze with 13 figures and two buildings – all of them contributing significantly to the impact of the tale he is telling.

At the far left stands the god Apollo; his role is important but only becomes apparent at the end of the story. Next comes the fountain-house. A young man is just placing his hydria beneath one spout; a girl stands on the other side waiting for her hydria to fill. She looks to the right and raises her arms in astonishment at what she sees. Beside her are three gods (Achilles' mother Thetis, Hermes and Athena), exerting an influence on the action, though presumably unseen by the mortals. In the centre Troilos is shown urging on his horses with all his might. The figure of Achilles is mostly lost, but even the single leg that has been preserved is telling. The foot has left the ground as the hero leaps forward to overtake the terrified boy. Polyxena runs in front of her brother; the hydria that she dropped in her fright lies overturned beneath the horses. Further to the right, the aged king of Troy, Priam, brow puckered, sits bent under the weight of his sorrows while his friend Antenor brings him this latest piece of bad news. At the extreme right we see two of Troilos' brothers emerging from the city gates, eager to avenge his murder.

The quality of Kleitias' work can be appreciated in a detail of Troilos himself (Fig. 52). The sensitive, precise drawing gives a vivid sense of the boy's fear, showing him with back arched, hair streaming, lips tight as he whips on his nervous, high-bred horses, racing fruitlessly against death. For, indeed, Troilos

52. Detail of Fig. 51.

did not escape. He fled to the sanctuary of Apollo and there was overtaken and brutally slain by Achilles. This deed outraged Apollo, for the sanctity of his shrine had been violated, and his stored-up anger against Achilles was finally appeased only when he had brought about the death of the hero.

Kleitias has given an epic breadth to his picture, weaving together insights into the bloody future with visions of an idyllic past in order to place the pursuit of Troilos within a wider context. Thus Apollo at the left hints at the death of Troilos and the vengeance that the god will take on his murderer, while the boy and girl at the fountain-house suggest the tranquil activities of common folk still undisturbed by war. The tone begins to change with the appearance of the three gods who encourage Achilles to a prodigious burst of speed allowing him to overtake galloping horses. The central scene of the life-and-death race between Achilles and Troilos is fraught with tension and drama – one would like to know what kind of emotional contribution was made by the fleeing Polyxena, whose skirt and feet alone are preserved. At the far right, we see the consequences of the horrors of war, the old king Priam, crushed by suffering, preparing to mourn the death of one child, while two others emerge from the city fully armed ready to join the fray – a poignant contrast with the peaceful scene at the fountain-house.

Narrow friezes like this require many figures to fill them. They encourage artists to choose generic subjects like processions, races, hunts, battles or revels that can be indefinitely expanded. When a specific myth is illustrated painters have to think it out in an extended form. Kleitias' excellence is revealed in the way he was able to give meaning to every element in his frieze.

The story of Troilos seemed particularly appropriate as decoration for a water jar (hydria) and Figs. 49, 50 and 53 are all hydriai. (Kleitias [Figs. 51-52] was decorating a different kind of vessel.)

Greek hydriai were normally equipped with three handles, a horizontal pair at the sides for lifting and a vertical one at the back for pouring (as can be seen in the pictures of hydriai on Figs 49-50). During the 6th century BC the shape was sharply articulated, with the lip of the vessel clearly set off from the neck, the neck from the shoulder, and the shoulder from the body. This offered vase painters two distinct fields for decoration: the almost square zone on the body and the long thin frieze on the shoulder. Figs. 49 and 50 are painted on the shoulders of hydriai.

Later potters preferred a hydria of a somewhat different shape, one in which neck, shoulder and body flow into one another in a sweeping continuous curve (Fig. 53). The uninterrupted curving surface of body and shoulder provided a single, rather upright, field for decoration. While artists faced with long narrow friezes had to think hard about how to expand a story in order to fill the space, artists confronted with more compact spaces had to devise some way to compress a story.

Fortunately, once a conventional form had been created, excerpts could effectively stand for the whole story. For instance, the image of a warrior crouching behind a fountain-house would be enough to call up the whole story of Achilles' ambush of Troilos. Similarly Achilles' pursuit of Troilos and Polyxena could also be abbreviated. Thus the artist of Fig. 53 has filled his space grandly with only a few large figures: Polyxena, at the far right, arms flailing, runs rapidly to the right, looking back in terror; Troilos, riding one horse and leading another, whips on his steed as he glances fearfully behind him. There is no room to show Achilles, nor is his presence really necessary: the effects of his attack are amply illustrated. Polyxena's hydria, which she has dropped in her flight, is of the old-fashioned shape. It smashes on the ground and the water pours out, just

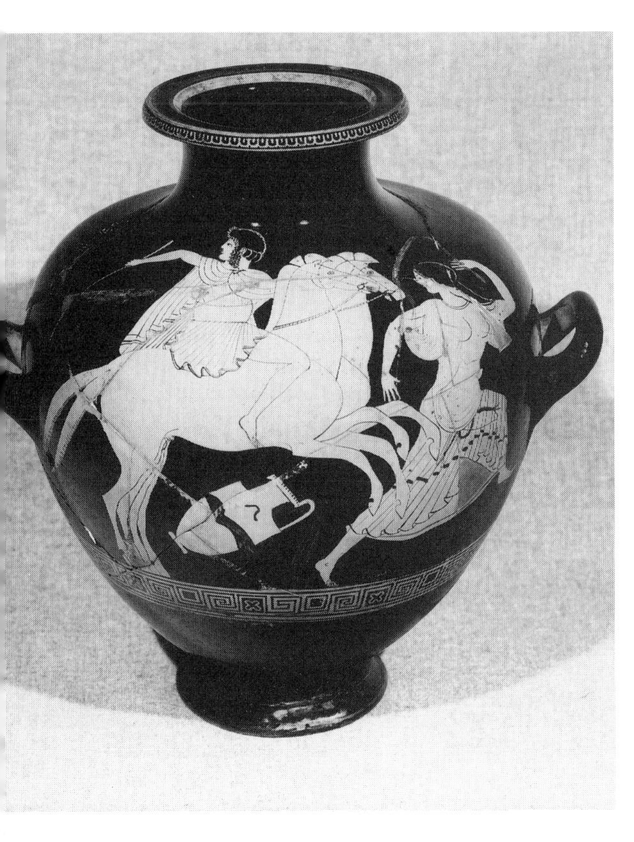

53. Troilos and Polyxena fleeing, Attic red-figure hydria, about 480 BC, by the Troilos Painter, London, British Museum.

as, all too soon, the blood of Troilos will be spilt.

*

Figures 49-52 are all examples of vase painting in the black-figure technique, a technique devised by vase painters in Corinth early in the 7th century BC and adopted by the Athenians late in the same century. It consisted of painting figures in black silhouette and articulating inner markings – and sometimes also contours – by means of incisions made with a sharp instrument before firing. A dark purplish-red was used for some details and white was added to indicate women's flesh or just for colouristic variety. The white has often flaked off in the course of time, leaving a dull black surface behind. Illustrations of the myths of the Trojan war were popular among black-figure vase painters. Many examples have already appeared in this book, some of them finer than others. Kleitias, for instance, made eloquent use of the technique, as can be seen in the expressive incision that characterises Troilos' intensity and his fright (Fig. 52). A generation later, another Athenian black-figure vase painter, Exekias, explored quieter moods but with no less impressive results (Figs 54 and 55): the complexity, precision and sheer virtuosity of Exekias' rendering of the embroidery on two heroes' cloaks and the fine texture of their beards and hair are absolutely breathtaking.

More than 150 vases have survived that show this subject – two warriors engrossed in playing a board game. In some cases the names of the warriors are inscribed: Achilles and Ajax. The earliest and the most beautiful of all these vases has not only the names of the heroes inscribed, but also their throws (Figs. 54 and 55): Achilles, to the left, has a 4, Ajax a 3. This image is exquisitely drawn and finely composed. This was Exekias' masterpiece and he signed his name as both painter and potter. He was a thoughtful artist who made his picture as rich in meaning as it was refined in meticulously engraved detail.

Achilles and Ajax were cousins and good friends. Ajax was the son of Telamon, who had fought successfully against Troy by the side of Herakles. He was, like Achilles, a bold and intrepid fighter and eager to match the achievements of his father.

The two warriors had much sympathy for each other. They were fighting men of comparable stature, each so confident in his own ability that neither feared to place his camp at the exposed extremes of the Greek lines, for, according to Homer:

54. Ajax and Achilles playing a game, Attic black-figure amphora, 540-530 BC, by Exekias, Vatican, Rome.

These two heroes had drawn up their shapely ships at the furthermost ends, trusting in their valour and the strength of their hands.

Homer *Iliad* 11, 7-9
(trans. Murray)

The symmetrical placement of the two heroes on either side of the gaming board provides a concise image within a restricted format of the location of their camps – equal and opposite at the two ends of the Greek encampment at Troy.

But though the placement of their camps may have been equal, the two heroes themselves were not. Achilles was always acknowledged to be the greatest of the Greek warriors; Ajax could only claim to be 'second only to Achilles'.

Exekias has delicately indicated Achilles' superiority not only by means of his higher throw in the game, but also by the way he is subtly made to dominate the picture: although Ajax and Achilles are about the same height, Achilles appears taller because he is wearing his helmet, while Ajax, bare-headed, has put his behind him, resting on his shield.

Exekias has sensitively adjusted the

55. Detail of Fig. 54.

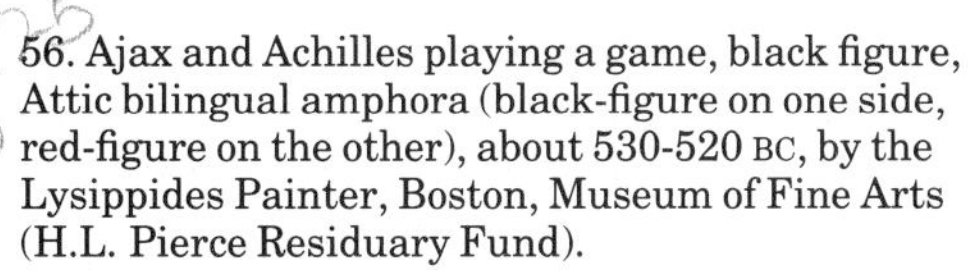

56. Ajax and Achilles playing a game, black figure, Attic bilingual amphora (black-figure on one side, red-figure on the other), about 530-520 BC, by the Lysippides Painter, Boston, Museum of Fine Arts (H.L. Pierce Residuary Fund).

57. Ajax and Achilles playing a game, red-figure, by the Andokides painter, the other side of Fig. 56.

composition to the shape of the vase (Fig. 54). Both heroes lean forward. Their hunched shoulders and gently inclined bodies contribute to the mood of the scene and also play an important part in the design. Exekias not only made the outlines of the heroes follow the outlines of the vessel, he also placed the spears, which they seem to hold so casually, in a position to lead the eye up to the top of the handles, and he has arranged the shields behind the heroes so that they continue the vertical line formed by the lower part of the handles.

The superb quality of Exekias' vase becomes apparent if it is compared with another, slightly later black-figure representation of the same subject (Fig. 56). This is a very respectable piece of work, with carefully controlled incision and sober design, but it is not a masterpiece, like that of Exekias. The later artist has chosen to stress the equality of the two heroes by showing them both bareheaded.

Another artist decorated the other side of this vase with the same subject, but he did so in another technique (Fig. 57). He did not paint the figures in silhouette, but left them in the natural colour of the vase and painted the background black instead. Details have been rendered with a brush, rather than being incised, and this has given them a new fluidity. The technique is called red-figure.

The inversion of the colour-scheme did not simply produce a reversal of the design: the use of a brush allowed more flexibility in drawing and the bold, light figures gave a greater impression of corporeality. These factors eventually encouraged the depiction of foreshortened limbs, complicated postures and the suggestion of space. Red-figure could also be developed into a fine vehicle for conveying subtle states of mind, and so red-figure artists, who also frequently illustrated the myths of the Trojan war, often chose episodes rich in psychological nuances (for instance, Figs. 11, 12, 23 and 43) in preference to those that were full of violent action. The red-figure technique was invented in Athens about 530 BC and quickly attracted many of the more gifted artists who were eager to explore the new possibilities that it offered. Black-figure vases, however, continued to be produced in large numbers well into the first quarter of the 5th century BC.

Notice that the red-figure artist of Fig. 57 has, like his black-figure counterpart on the other side of the vase, stressed the equality of the two heroes, but rather than showing them both bareheaded, he has shown them both helmeted. The subtle asymmetry so effectively employed by Exekias (Fig. 55) apparently did not appeal to other artists; out of the scores of representations of this scene the rule that either both heroes are bareheaded or both are helmeted is adhered to virtually without exception.

Some decades after Exekias first painted the theme a new variation was introduced: the goddess Athena was shown standing between the two heroes. In Fig. 58 not only are the two heroes labelled, but so, too, is Athena, even though she is unmistakably characterised by her helmet and aegis. Here, too, both heroes call out their throws, a 4 for Achilles, only a 2 for Ajax. Both heroes are bareheaded.

The addition of Athena proved to be a very popular innovation and the vast majority of the surviving representations include her. Artists may have liked the central accent that her standing figure provided. She seems to be gesticulating energetically, her attention focused more on Achilles than Ajax, but there is little consensus as to exactly what her gesture signifies.

The images of Ajax and Achilles playing a game that we have looked at so far have all been contained within a space that has

58. Ajax and Achilles playing a game with Athena between them, Attic black-figure lekythos, about 500 BC, Circle of the Edinburgh Painter, Boston, Museum of Fine Arts (Perkins Collection).

restricted the picture to no more than three figures and a pair of framing shields. The broad exteriors of Greek stemmed cups (*kylikes*), however, were rather like long narrow friezes and so required the addition of more figures. Fig. 59 illustrates the solution that was preferred by artists decorating this sort of field: Athena stands in the centre; the two heroes, both helmeted, are intent on their game; flanking them, warriors are engaged in fighting.

Some scholars have thought that this picture shows Athena alerting the two heroes to the battle raging around them. They suggest that there was once a story that told how when Ajax and Achilles were on guard-duty, they began to play a

59. Ajax and Achilles playing a game with Athena between them and warriors fighting at each side, Attic red-figure cup exterior, late 6th century BC, by Epiktetos, Aberdeen 744 and Florence B 20.

game in order to pass the time and eventually became so engrossed in it that they missed the alarm and were in imminent danger of being overrun by the enemy had it not been for the timely intervention of the goddess Athena. These scholars believe that some literary work (now lost) told this tale and that artists could represent it in its entirety only when decorating long friezes (Fig. 59), but that they liked to portray excerpts of it (Figs. 55-58) when space did not permit such an extended narrative.

It is possible that this is true, but it is also possible that it is not. No trace of such a story exists in surviving literature, though, of course, many tales may have circulated in antiquity which have not come down to us. Nevertheless, it is important to remember that the fact that the story fits the pictures provides no proof; the story was invented by the scholars precisely in order to do just that!

Other scholars believe that no story need ever have existed in verbal form and that the theme of the game-playing heroes was a creation not of poets but of visual artists.

Myths in antiquity were never considered immutably fixed. The outcome of a myth may have been generally accepted, but its development could be elaborated at will. We have seen how freely the story of the Judgement of Paris or of the beautiful Helen could be treated by different artists – both visual and verbal. Poets were always uninhibited in the way they treated myth. Artists must have felt equally free to expand familiar episodes or even to invent new ones. Like poets, painters steeped in mythology could develop their own feelings about heroic characters and their activities. Exekias, for example, could have arrived at an image of Ajax and Achilles playing a game (Figs. 54-55) simply by doodling mentally with ideas about the tedious length of the siege of Troy and the boredom of heroes accustomed to action during periods of enforced inactivity. No poem was needed, not even a story told by the fireside.

Ajax and Achilles playing a game, once drawn, caught the fancy of other artists. They might have avoided the asymmetry introduced by Exekias either on compositional grounds – not everybody could produce a harmonious picture with only one hero helmeted – or because they felt the similarities between the heroes were greater than the differences (Figs. 56 and 57).

After a while, however, a few artists might have thought that Achilles ought to be shown with some indication of his greater importance, or, perhaps, it came to be felt that the equalisation of the two heroes had gone too far and that some element ought to distinguish between them and perhaps favour one over the other. Thus Athena was introduced, shown turning toward Achilles (Fig. 58). This innovation, which provided a strong central accent for the composition, made the theme much more attractive to a great number of artists.

The need to fill the long, low frieze of a cup exterior was probably what prompted some vase painters to add warriors flanking the players; after all, the protagonists were in armour and so it could be assumed that they were not far from the scene of battle. Athena might be present (as in Fig. 59) or absent; in any case the space had been decorated effectively and that was what mattered.

Not everybody is persuaded that this sort of visual explanation is as plausible as the theory that such vases illustrate some (lost) pre-existing story, but it seems a pity to deny that artists could sometimes speak as independently and creatively in images as poets could in words.

5

The Anger of Achilles

By the tenth year of the war the Greeks were still laying siege to powerful Troy, but they had already captured and laid waste many cities in the neighbourhood. When a city was sacked, the spoils were divided up and the treasures distributed, the best of them going to the leaders of the army. Agamemnon, as commander-in-chief, always came out particularly well.

Captured women were allotted like other goods. Some of them were highly prized, being seen as special marks of distinction – and this could occasionally present problems.

Chryseis, the daughter of a priest of Apollo, was awarded to Agamemnon. He was extremely pleased, preferring her, as he admitted himself, to his lawful wife Klytaimnestra. But Chryseis' father also valued the girl and tried to ransom her, offering splendid gifts in return. Agamemnon refused the offer and the angry priest prayed to Apollo to avenge his disappointment by sending a plague upon the Greeks. For nine days the plague raged, and on the tenth Achilles called an assembly. He wanted to find out what had caused the plague so that appropriate measures could be taken to put an end to it. The seer Kalchas knew well enough what the trouble was, but he knew, too, that it was unwise to offend a king. Only when Achilles promised him full protection did he declare that if Agamemnon were to return Chryseis to her father, Apollo would be appeased and the plague would cease.

The solution seemed obvious, but Agamemnon was reluctant to part with his prize without ensuring that he would be properly compensated. It was not just that he liked the girl; it was also that he felt it would be a disgrace if he were the only one of the leaders deprived of the mark of honour that she represented.

Achilles pointed out that there were no spare prizes available in the camp, but that if Agamemnon gave up the girl now, he would be amply compensated later when Troy was captured. He put his reasonable observation in rather intemperate language and Agamemnon, becoming increasingly touchy about his position, insisted that he would not tolerate being singled out for humiliation in this way. He swore that once he had returned the girl to her father, if the Greeks did not voluntarily provide him with what he considered to be a prize of equal value, he would help himself to the prize of one of the other leaders.

Tempers rose. Sharp words were exchanged. It looked as if the issue would come to blows, and, indeed, Achilles was actually in the process of drawing his sword from its scabbard, when the goddess Athena intervened (Fig. 60).

*

Until now we have seen artists illustrating stories that they knew intimately but which are known to us usually only

60. Achilles confronting Agamemnon restrained by Athena, Roman mosaic from Pompeii, second half of the 1st century AD, Naples, Museo Nazionale.

obliquely through allusions, asides, dry summaries or sometimes, luckily, through little vignettes. Fig. 60 is the first example in this book of an illustration probably drawn from a literary source that we know just as much about as the Roman artist who made the mosaic – or maybe even more.

The scene between Achilles and Agamemnon and the chain of events that their dispute set into motion are lit up for us because they were the subject of Homer's great epic poem the *Iliad*. The *Iliad*, which takes its title from 'Ilios', an alternative name for the city of Troy, has come down to us substantially in its original form.

The theme of the *Iliad* is announced in the first line: the anger of Achilles. This anger of Achilles arose out of the incident described above and out of its consequences.

Homer gives a vivid picture of the war of words between Achilles and Agamemnon. At its climax, Achilles is undecided whether he should draw his sword and kill Agamemnon on the spot or whether he should restrain himself. Homer recounts:

> While he was pondering this in his mind and his heart, and was pulling his great sword from the scabbard, ... Athena came up behind him and caught the son of Peleus by his yellow hair ...
>
> Homer *Iliad* I, 193-195
> (trans. Hammond)

The Roman mosaicist (Fig. 60) has shown the bearded Agamemnon, seated on a kingly throne, holding his regal sceptre, head raised as he addresses the impetuous young Achilles who lunges towards him menacingly, his hand upon the hilt of his sword. At the same moment, Athena appears behind Achilles. Much of her figure has been lost owing to damage to the mosaic, but one can still see clearly how she has grasped Achilles by the hair.

The image looks so much like a literal illustration of the poem that one begins to wonder if the mosaicist actually had the text before him as he placed his tiny stones within their setting. If this were so, it is perhaps a little disappointing that the scene, for all its literalness, is so drab.

But in fact it is really more likely that the artist had a book of pictures rather than a book of words in front of him. We have already seen an example of how a famous type could be re-used in later images (Figs. 19, 21 and 22 and p. 30) and here we see again how craftsmen could adopt or adapt celebrated compositions which were transmitted by means of the copy-books which apparently circulated through many workshops.

A fragment of a painting from Pompeii (Fig. 61) is clearly derived from the same source but is much livelier: Achilles' movement is more convincing, the swirl of Athena's drapery and the pull of her body away from Achilles are much more suggestive of the haste with which she has come and the urgency of the restraint she exerts. The Pompeian painter seems to be much closer to the spirit of the text than the mosaicist, though he too, of course, was probably only re-working a composition originally formulated by a Greek artist centuries earlier.

61. Achilles about to draw his sword, restrained by Athena, fragment of a Roman painting from Pompeii, second half of the 1st century AD, Naples, Museo Nazionale.

*

In the *Iliad*, Athena persuaded Achilles not to attack Agamemnon with his sword, but to attack him with words instead. Agamemnon, stung, swore to punish Achilles for his bold tongue by taking *his* prize-of-honour, a girl called Briseis, to replace Chryseis, whom he finally consented to give up. Thus, after Chryseis had been delivered back to her father and the plague effectively stopped, Agamemnon sent two heralds to collect Briseis from Achilles. Homer says:

> They found him [Achilles] by his hut and his black ship, sitting idle: and Achilles had no joy in seeing them. They stood there silent, without word or question, in fear and respect for the king. But he understood their purpose in his mind, and spoke to them: 'Welcome, heralds, messengers of Zeus and of men. Come closer. It is not you I blame, but Agamemnon, who has sent you here for the girl Briseis. Come, lord Patroklos, bring the girl out and give her to them for the taking ...'
>
> So he spoke, and Patroklos did as his dear friend told him. He brought the beautiful Briseis out of the hut, and gave her to the heralds to take. They went back again to the ships of the Achaians [Greeks], and the woman went with them, reluctant.
>
> Homer *Iliad* 1, 328-349 (trans. Hammond)

62. Briseis taken from Achilles, Roman painting, probably based on a 4th century BC Greek original, third quarter of the 1st century AD, Naples, Museo Nazionale, from Pompeii.

Once again a Roman painting (Fig. 62) inspired by an older Greek masterpiece seems to offer a literal, but rather soulless, illustration of the scene. Achilles, in the centre, is seated before his hut making an emphatic gesture to signify that Briseis should be given to the heralds. Patroklos, his back turned to us, gently leads the girl forward. At the right, Briseis, to indicate her reluctance, wipes a tear from her eye.

Illustrating a scene as literally as possible may seem to show a profound respect for a text, but translating moving words into bland images is not necessarily getting to the heart of the matter.

Agamemnon's arrogant gesture in robbing Achilles of this girl, a prize bestowed on him as a mark of honour by the troops, was the flash-point which generated that baleful anger of Achilles which determined the course of events which are chronicled with unparalleled dramatic power in the *Iliad*.

A Greek vase painter early in the 5th century BC decorated the exterior of a cup with a scene showing the removal of Briseis (Fig. 63). The girl moves with slow dignity between her two escorts, while two men flanking the hut of Achilles appear to contemplate the consequences of this event. The hut itself is economically indicated by two columns over which some striped drapery is swathed. It is a striking setting which frames the figure of Achilles, seated, closed in on himself, his cloak over his head, muffled in his rage and humiliation. The five standing figures are emotionally muted. All attention, visually and psychologically, is focused on the grieving Achilles. Certainly this is a much less literal illustration of the Homeric passage than Fig. 62, but it is one that reveals more tellingly the core of the story.

Once the girl had been removed, Achilles called his mother Thetis to him. To her he confided his anger at having his prize-of-honour so summarily and unjustly taken from him and his resolve to withdraw from the fighting in order to make the Greeks see the folly of having treated their most brilliant warrior so shabbily. Just to make sure that his value was properly appreciated, he begged his mother to persuade Zeus to make things go badly for the Greeks during his absence from the battle.

*

The *Iliad* is full of battles, fierce fighting, brutal killings, blood and gore, but also heroism, loyalty and devotion. There are countless descriptions of confrontations, when individual warriors met one another in a trial of skill and valour. Most such meetings took place by chance, but on two occasions a formal challenge was

63. Briseis taken from Achilles, Attic red-figure cup exterior, about 480 BC, by the Briseis Painter, London, British Museum.

issued. In the third book of the *Iliad*, Paris called for a truce so that he and Menelaos could decide by means of single combat to whom the lovely Helen should belong. Menelaos eventually gained the upper hand and was very near finishing Paris off when Aphrodite intervened to rescue her protégé and whisk him away to his sweet-scented bedroom. She then summoned Helen and ordered her to go to Paris. Helen went reluctantly and only under pressure from the goddess, for she had begun to yearn for her former husband and her home and the family she had abandoned so many years before in the first flush of her romance with Paris. Now, when Aphrodite obliged her to sit down obediently opposite Paris, Helen vented her feelings by speaking freely – and hurtfully – to her lover:

'You came back from the fighting, then. I wish you had died there, brought down by a man of strength, who was once my husband. Oh, before now you used to boast that you were superior to the warrior Menelaos in strength and power of hand and spear. Well, go now, challenge the warrior Menelaos to fight you again face to face. No, I would advise you to stop now, and not pit yourself against fair-haired Menelaos in warfare or combat without thinking – you might well be brought down by his spear.'

Homer *Iliad* 3, 428-436
(trans. Hammond)

Helen's chiding tone and her prickly relationship with Paris, as portrayed here, contrast with Homer's depiction of the relationship of Paris' brother, Hektor, with his wife Andromache. Hektor was the most valiant of Priam's sons, a gallant defender of the city and an outstanding warrior. In the sixth book of the *Iliad* Homer tells how he left the battlefield briefly to visit the city and took this opportunity to look in on his wife. He did not find her at home, because, hearing rumours of a great Greek victory, she had rushed to the battlements to see for herself. Hektor strode off to meet her and when he

> reached the Skaian gates … there came running to him his dowered wife, Andromache … . She came running up to him and with her there went a maid carrying at her breast their innocent child, no more than a baby, Hektor's only beloved son, shining lovely as a star. … Hektor looked at his son and smiled in silence. Andromache came close to him with her tears falling, and took his hand and spoke to him: 'Poor dear man, your own brave spirit will destroy you, and you have no pity for your baby son and for me your doomed wife, who will soon be your widow. Soon the Achaians [Greeks] will mass an attack on you and kill you. And for me then, when I lose you, it would be better to sink down under the earth. There will be no other comfort left for me, when you have met your fate, only misery … Please, feel pity for us, stay here on the battlements, so you do not make an orphan of your child and your wife a widow … .'
>
> Then great Hektor of the glinting helm answered her: 'Wife, all that you say is surely in my mind also. But I would feel terrible shame before the men of Troy and the women of Troy with their trailing dresses, if like a coward I skulk away from the fighting. Nor is that what my own heart urges, because I have learnt always to be brave and to fight in the forefront of the Trojans, winning great glory for my father and for myself. One thing I know well in my heart and in my mind: the day will come when sacred Ilios [Troy] shall be destroyed, and Priam and the people of Priam of the fine ash spear. But the pain I feel for the suffering to come is less for the people of Troy, less even for Hekabe and king Priam and my brothers, the many brave brothers who will fall in the dust at the hands of our enemies, than my pain for you, when one of the bronze-clad Achaians carries you away in tears and takes away the day of your freedom: and you will live in Argos, weaving at the loom at another woman's command, and carrying water from a foreign spring … much against your will, but compulsion will lie harsh upon you. And someone seeing you with your tears falling will say: "This is the wife of Hektor, who was always the best warrior of the horse-taming Trojans, when they were fighting over Ilios." That is what they will say: and for you there will be renewed misery, that you have lost such a husband to protect you from the day of slavery. But may I be dead and heaped earth upon me, before I hear your screams and the sound of you being dragged away.'
>
> So speaking glorious Hektor reached out to take his son. But the child shrank back crying against the breast of his girdled nurse, terrified at the sight of his own father, frightened by the bronze and the crest of the horse-hair, as he saw it nodding dreadfully from the top of the helmet. His dear father and his honoured mother laughed aloud at this, and glorious Hektor took the helmet straight from his head and laid it gleaming bright on the ground. Then he kissed his dear son and dandled him in his arms, and said in prayer to Zeus and the other gods: 'Zeus and you other gods, grant that this my son may become, as I have been, pre-eminent among the Trojans, as strong and brave as I, and may he rule in strength over Ilios. And let people say, as he returns from the fighting: "This man is better by far than his father. May he carry home the bloody spoils of the enemy he has killed, and bring joy to his mother." '
>
> So speaking he placed his son in his dear wife's arms. She took him to her scented breast, smiling with tears in her eyes. Her husband saw the tears and was moved to pity. He stroked her with his hand, and spoke to her, saying: 'Poor wife, please do not let your heart be too distressed. No man will send me down to Hades before my fated time …'
>
> Homer *Iliad* 6, 392-487
> (trans. Hammond)

The tenderness of the encounter stands out amid the bloodshed; the scene is a memorable one.

The contrast between the relationship of Helen and Paris sketched in the third book of the *Iliad* and that of Hektor and Andromache in the sixth book of the *Iliad* impressed a Greek vase painter who juxtaposed the two couples on a black-figure bowl (Fig. 64). The four protagonists have their names inscribed beside them. At the far left stands Helen, her head turned away from the lightly-armed Paris, who approaches her holding the bow which he can use so effectively in battle. Back to back with Paris stands Andromache. She looks Hektor fully in the face and reaches out one hand to touch him. Hektor, who occupies the very centre of the composition, is the epitome of a heavily-armed warrior. He has greaves strapped to his legs, a cuirass protecting his chest, and a round shield on his arm. He wears a helmet on his head, the nodding plume of which penetrates the decorative border at the top of the picture.

To the right, Hektor's squire sits upon one horse and holds another one in readiness for the departing hero.

Visually the two standing couples are not very expressive, but to anyone who has Homer's verses ringing in his ears, the image of Helen, closely wrapped in her cloak and turning away from her lover as opposed to Andromache, who, though she has her head modestly veiled, holds her cloak open as she faces her husband, speaks volumes.

Sometimes pictures can be eloquent all on their own, but at other times we have to know what their creator had in mind before we can appreciate their full impact.

*

Paris challenged Menelaos specifically to single combat in the third book of the *Iliad*. In the seventh book, his brother Hektor issued a general challenge to any

64. Helen and Paris; Andromache and Hektor, Chalcidian black-figure krater, about 540-530 BC, by the Inscription Painter, Würzburg, Martin von Wagner Museum.

one of the Greeks to meet him in single combat. Nine of the foremost warriors drew lots for the honour – and the danger – of confronting Hektor, and the lot fell to the mighty Ajax. The two heroes fought impressively but the conflict was still undecided when night closed in and the heralds from both sides intervened to separate them. As they parted, Hektor said to Ajax:

> 'But come, let us both give each other glorious gifts, so that people will say, both Achaians [Greeks] and Trojans: "These two fought together in rivalry that ate at their hearts, and then when they parted were joined in friendship." '
>
> So speaking he fetched a sword with a silver-nailed hilt and gave it to Aias, together with its sheath and baldric of well-cut leather: and Aias gave him a

belt brilliant with purple. And so they parted.

Homer *Iliad* 7, 299-306
(trans. Hammond)

Thus the two heroes went their separate ways on courteous terms.

An early 5th century BC artist, intrigued by the indecisive outcome of this encounter which began so full of menace and ended so tamely, painted the two warriors on opposite sides of a vase. Each is shown holding the gift he has received conspicuously in his right hand, but each, as he is led away by an older companion, looks back at the other as if some business were still left unfinished (Fig. 65). In fact, the two did meet again on the field of battle and fought with equal valour, but neither one ever succeeded in inflicting a fatal injury upon the other. The sword and the belt, however, gave rise to a tradition which suggested that a malign influence eventually worked its way through these gifts exchanged by enemies, however gallantly they may have been given in good faith.

65. Ajax and Hektor exchange gifts, Attic red-figure amphora, about 480 BC, by the Kleophrades Painter, Würzburg, Martin von Wagner Museum.

Ajax was not the only Greek hero who fought bravely while Achilles skulked in and around his hut nursing his injured pride. Nevertheless, Achilles' absence began to tell, and the tide of battle began to turn against the Greeks. Agamemnon saw this and began sorely to regret the offence he had given to Achilles. Eager to put matters right before the whole expedition was overcome by disaster, he was prepared to try to make amends and to offer rich gifts in compensation.

A deputation was carefully chosen to bring Agamemnon's proposals to Achilles. Three men were selected: the articulate and persuasive Odysseus, the blunt Ajax – a warrior after Achilles' own heart – and the aged Phoinix, who had cared for Achilles ever since he was a baby. When the emissaries arrived at Achilles' encampment, they found Achilles diverting himself by playing the lyre and singing of the deeds of famous men. Once again we see how the lessons learned in youth from the pedagogic centaur (see

66. The Embassy to Achilles, Attic red-figure stamnos, about 480 BC, by the Triptolemus Painter, Swiss private collection, on loan to the Antikenmuseum, Basel.

Fig. 19) served Achilles well in adulthood.

When he became aware of the deputation, Achilles received the men warmly, for he was delighted to see these three treasured friends. The emissaries then proceeded to present the case for a reconciliation, each in terms of his own character and his relationship to Achilles, but none of them could induce Achilles to accept either Agamemnon's bid for reconciliation or his gifts. Achilles' anger had now bitten too deeply to allow him to relent. He would concede no more than that he and his troops would not sail away immediately and hinted darkly that Hektor would meet his match should he ever succeed in setting fire to the fleet and penetrating to Achilles' own encampment.

Achilles' anger had been justifiable up to this point, but in refusing the generous reparations offered by Agamemnon, he had finally put himself in the wrong. The price he eventually had to pay for this indulgence of his grievance turned out to be a terrible one.

The Embassy to Achilles was a popular subject with Athenian red-figure vase painters in the early 5th century BC (Fig. 66). Their interest focused on the central group of Odysseus and Achilles and the contrast between these two seated figures: Odysseus, urbane, suave and relaxed, scantily draped but equipped with the traveller's hat which was often used to identify him, and Achilles, closed in on himself, brooding, enveloped in the cloak that covers his head and engulfs his body, the lyre nowhere in sight. The two figures were so powerfully characterised that even when they were reduced to mere formulae in the hands of less gifted artists, they still retained a very considerable emotional impact.

Illustrations of what appear to be Homeric scenes, like Fig. 66, often turn out not to have actually been derived directly from the *Iliad*. Homeric poetry provided the inspiration for many artists, both visual and verbal, and the renowned 5th century BC playwright Aeschylus is supposed to have once declared that his own splendid tragedies were mere 'slices from Homer's banquet'.

Many poems and plays expanded on episodes briefly recounted or merely alluded to in the *Iliad* and many illustrations are based on these later developments from the epic tradition. This appears to have been the case with the cluster of vase paintings near the beginning of the 5th century BC which showed the Embassy to Achilles, for it was just about this time that Aeschylus produced a tragedy (now lost) which dealt with this very theme. Aeschylus' play featured a sullen, silent Achilles, reluctant to respond to the clever Odysseus, who appeared, unaccompanied by the other two, to plead the Greeks' case.

Certainly the most haunting image in illustrations of the Embassy to Achilles is that of Achilles himself. The figure lacks eloquence of contour but has an emotional immediacy that belies its apparent simplicity. It was a brilliant and subtle idea to show grief in terms of this sort of muffled figure, the body almost lumpishly obscured by the drapery. This type – the mourning Achilles – seems to have been invented by artists who had been inspired by the Aeschylean tragedy in the early 5th century BC. The characterisation appeared so apt that the painter of the cup showing Briseis taken away from Achilles (Fig. 63) intelligently adapted it for his own purposes.

Vase painters often introduced supplementary figures either to fill up the available space or to amplify the narrative. In adding these, artists illustrating the Embassy to Achilles were probably recalling the Homeric picture of the scene, producing, therefore, a sort of composite illustration of the epic and the tragic versions of the story. Thus, the aged Phoinix was frequently included; he appears at the far right in Fig. 66. Patroklos, Achilles' great friend and companion, might be shown, or Ajax, the third member of the embassy. In Fig. 66 the man standing at the far left, backing up Odysseus, certainly looks as if he should be Ajax, but, puzzlingly, he is inscribed 'Diomedes'. There is little doubt that the position fits Ajax and so it seems likely that the vase painter just made a mistake when he wrote in the wrong name. Why did he do it?

Diomedes was one of the boldest of the Greek warriors. According to Homer he spoke just before the embassy was proposed and just after it returned, and this may have brought him to the artist's mind. More important, however, may have been Diomedes' relationship with Odysseus. He often worked in partnership with Odysseus on special expeditions – for instance, in fetching Achilles from Skyros (Fig. 21 and p. 29). Perhaps this association occurred to the vase painter when he drew the man behind Odysseus; Odysseus' relations with Ajax were, on the whole, not nearly as cordial. In an absent-minded moment, the artist may have let his knowledge of the mythological characters and their relationships in other contexts outweigh the specific incident that he was illustrating. After all, he was drawing imagery from both epic and theatre, with no single text dominating his imagination, and it was easy to make a mistake when writing a name.

*

The Greeks were disappointed to hear of the unsatisfactory outcome of the mission to Achilles, but they were resigned to the fact that the fighting had to go on. The leaders were anxious to know what the Trojans planned to do next. That night they decided that some brave soul should go out and reconnoitre. Diomedes promptly volunteered, but declared that he would feel more confident if another hero were to accompany him. Many now stepped forward. From among them, Diomedes chose Odysseus.

On the Trojan side a similar project was taking shape. The Trojan Dolon undertook the task. Equipping himself with a bow and a spear and wearing a wolf's pelt over his shoulders and a marten's skin on his head, he set out to spy on the Greek camp. It was not long before he was spotted by Odysseus and Diomedes.

A South Italian vase painter has wittily portrayed the moment when the hapless Trojan is trapped between the two wily Greeks (Fig. 67). Red-figure vase paintings conventionally had a black background, but the convention here is given a

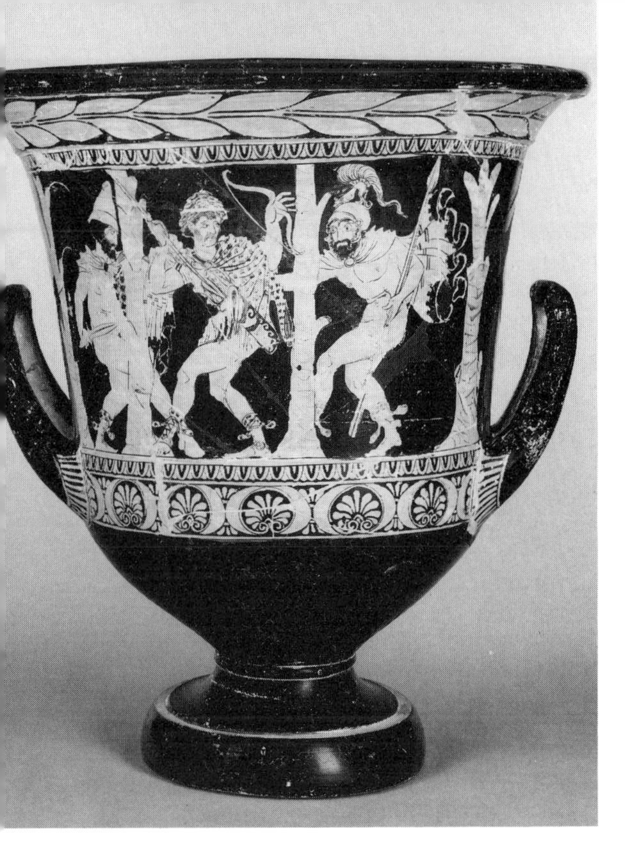

67. Odysseus and Diomedes ambush Dolon, Lucanian red-figure calyx krater, 390-380 BC, by the Dolon Painter, London, British Museum.

fresh, meaningful edge, for the ambush of Dolon took place at night, and the black background is wonderfully suggestive of that fact. The artist has shown the three protagonists weaving through the trees in the dark, Diomedes, to the right, tip-toeing in step with Dolon, the repetition of poses dance-like. But the hint of pantomime takes on sinister overtones as Odysseus, sword at the ready, closes in on the luckless Trojan from the left.

The night expedition proved a success for the Greeks, but otherwise the war went from bad to worse. Achilles noted this with satisfaction. As he watched the discomfiture of the Greeks, Achilles became curious about the identity of one of the heroes he observed being carried away from the field of battle. He sent Patroklos to find it out. The gentle Patroklos was shocked to see how many of the leading men had been wounded and how badly the Greeks were faring. He was, therefore, pleased to comply when the sage old warrior Nestor asked him to beg Achilles to give some aid to his hard-pressed comrades. If Achilles did not wish to enter the fray himself, Nestor suggested that he lend Patroklos his armour and send him out into battle with Achilles' fresh troops. This would at least give some respite to the sadly harried Greeks.

Achilles was touched by Patroklos' pleas and consented to do what he asked. He tenderly equipped Patroklos with his own glorious armour and gave him careful and explicit instructions to relieve the Greeks from their present danger – by this time the Trojans had already penetrated as far as the Greek ships and were about to set them alight – but not to pursue the Trojans to the very walls of their city.

Patroklos set off with determination. One Trojan hero after another fell to his onslaught, and intoxicated with his success he carried on courageously beyond the limits that Achilles had set for him.

Patroklos seemed to be sweeping all before him when the bravest of the Trojan allies made a stand against him. This was Sarpedon, leader of the Lycians and a son of the god Zeus. Zeus himself saw what was about to happen and was distressed, but his wife Hera discouraged him from trying to interfere with the course of destiny. She suggested that he leave Sarpedon to his fate, but that after he had been killed Zeus should honour him by ordering Sleep and Death to carry his body out of the battle and away to his home in Lycia where his kinsmen would give him a dignified burial and erect a monument to his memory.

Thus Patroklos duly triumphed over Sarpedon and slew him. Zeus ensured that a prolonged and bloody fight was waged over his fallen son. Finally, however, he instructed Apollo to take the body out of range, wash it with running

68. Sleep and Death (supervised by Hermes) carry the body of Sarpedon off the field of battle to Lycia, Attic red-figure calyx krater, 520-510 BC, by Euphronios, New York, Metropolitan Museum of Art (Bequest of Joseph H. Durkee, Gift of Darius Ogden Mills, and Gift of C. Ruxton Love).

water and wrap it in an imperishable robe, preparatory to handing it over to Sleep and Death to carry back to Lycia.

The late 6th century BC Athenian vase painter, who signed his name as Euphronios, has transformed the Homeric narrative into an impressive tableau on one side of a large bowl (Fig. 68). Euphronios was particularly interested in the portrayal of anatomy, and so he omitted the imperishable robe that was supposed to cover the body and instead lovingly drew in the detailed forms of the heroic nude figure. Blood pours from the wounds, while the fighting man's once powerful hands hang limply on the ground. Euphronios was successful in showing the hero's lower left leg persuasively foreshortened in front view, but less successful in depicting the right shoulder drooping lifelessly across the frontal view of the chest. The effort, however, was a brave one. These were heroic days in the struggle to render the human body in its full three-dimensional complexity on the curving surface of a vessel.

Sleep and Death are here portrayed as twin brothers, barely distinguishable but for the darker corselet of Death and the names inscribed beside each of the figures. Sleep and Death, like Eris, are personifications, abstract ideas for which the artist had to devise a suitable form. Euphronios imagined them dressed as warriors but equipped with wings so that they could fly off with their massive burden.

Though Apollo looms large in Homer's narrative, he does not appear in Euphronios' picture. Instead Hermes, who has no role in this part of the *Iliad*, stands behind Sarpedon's body, directing the action. Hermes was the god who guided the souls of the dead to Hades, and so it must have seemed natural to Euphronios for him to participate in the action. Euphronios was not slavishly following the verses of the poem but creating his own immediate vision of a heroic incident. A contemporary poet may have done the same and, as we have seen, the strands of influence and inspiration, rooted in Homeric poetry but flowering luxuriantly throughout classical antiquity, are difficult to disentangle.

Patroklos fought on irrepressibly, right up to the gates of Troy, and then he was overtaken by the grim fate that awaited him. Smitten first by the god Apollo, wounded next by the Trojan Euphorbos, he was finally killed by Hektor. Hektor, elated and triumphant, then stripped him of his arms, those glorious arms that had been lent to Patroklos by Achilles.

Patroklos' death was a great blow to the Greeks, for his unusual combination of bravery and gentleness had made him loved not only by Achilles but also by the rest of the Greek leaders. They made a valiant stand over his naked body. Menelaos particularly distinguished himself at this juncture, a fact that no doubt

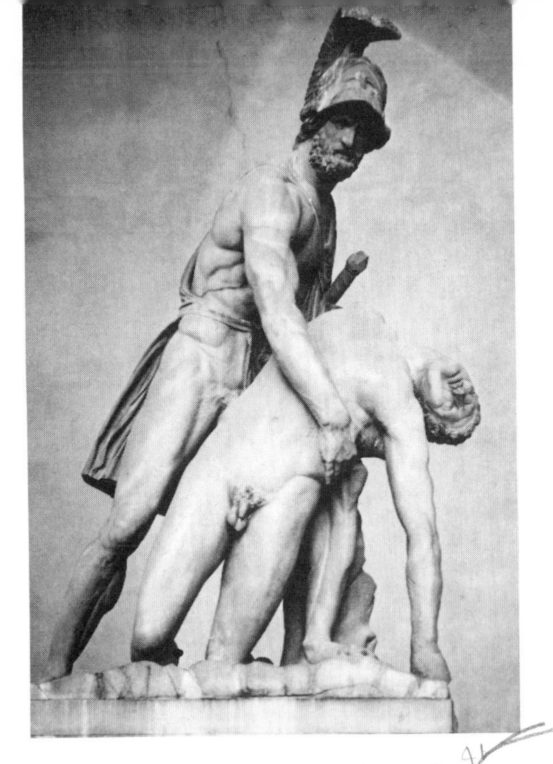

69. Menelaos with the body of Patroklos, a Roman copy of a bronze group made in the Hellenistic period, Florence, Loggia dei Lanzi.

inspired a gifted Hellenistic sculptor to compose an elegant, complex group in bronze showing Menelaos with the body of Patroklos. The original group has been lost, but copies made in marble by Roman artists can still give us an idea of what the complete group looked like (Fig. 69).

The two figures are locked together in a tight pyramidal group bounded, in the front view, on one side by Menelaos' right leg and on the other by Patroklos' hanging left arm. Menelaos grasps the body of Patroklos across the chest, his taut, active arm parallel to and contrasting with the limp, pendant arm of his comrade. Similarly Menelaos' vigorous, well muscled leg accentuates the lifelessness of Patroklos' right thigh. Formally the limbs of the living and the dead are parallel and the two pairs of diagonals impose a simple pattern on the complex group, giving it a harmony and beauty of line that complements the poignancy of the subject.

Fighting over the body of Patroklos was fierce and prolonged, but finally Menelaos with the help of another hero managed to carry the body of Patroklos, stripped of its armour, off the field of battle. It may have been this scene that the painter of a red-figure bowl had in mind when he drew what might at first seem a rather unexceptional incident in the course of heroic combat (Fig. 70). Five warriors hover about a dead comrade. Two lift the body and one stands behind it. The body is covered by a thin piece of cloth. The dead man's eyes are closed pathetically in death; his long hair, unrestrained by a helmet, hangs lifelessly. What particularly distinguishes this otherwise generic scene are the intensity of feeling manifested by the surviving warriors and the detail of a small armed figure leaping away from, but looking back at, the dead hero. This must be the artist's attempt to show the spirit of the dead man, regretfully departing from his body.

Before he died, Patroklos was able to gasp out a few words warning Hektor that he, too, had but a short time to live before

70. Patroklos (?) carried off the field of battle, Attic red-figure calyx krater, about 500 BC, by a painter of the Pezzino Group, Agrigento, Museo Nazionale.

he was to be struck down by Death and Destiny, slain by the hands of Achilles. Then, Homer explains,

> As he spoke the end of death enfolded him: and his spirit flitted from his body and went on the way to Hades, weeping for its fate, and the youth and manhood it must leave.
>
> Homer *Iliad* 16, 855-857
> (trans. Hammond)

Homer paints many pathetic pictures of men dying in battle, but only twice does he mention the grieving spirit that departs from the body: when he describes the death of Patroklos and when he describes the death of Hektor.

After he killed Patroklos, Hektor stripped him of his armour. He then took off his own armour, gave it to his men to take back to Troy, and

> put on the immortal armour of Achilles son of Peleus ... Zeus saw him and shook his head and said 'Poor wretch, death is not in your thought at all, and it is now coming close to you. You are dressing in the immortal armour of the best of men, a man all others fear. And you have now killed this man's friend, who was kind and strong, and you have taken the armour from his head and shoulders, wrongly. But for the moment I shall grant you great power, in recompense for what will happen – you will never return home from the fighting, for Andromache to take from you the famous armour of the son of Peleus.'
>
> Homer *Iliad* 17, 194-208
> (trans. Hammond)

Thus Hektor wore Achilles' armour and fought on bravely and Achilles, back in his camp, sat and waited for news of Patroklos.

6

The Anguish of Achilles

Achilles was shattered when he heard that Patroklos had been killed. The removal of Briseis had been a blow to his pride, but the death of Patroklos was a blow to his heart.

Grief, anguish and the thirst for revenge overwhelmed Achilles. When his mother rose from the sea along with her Nereid sisters in response to his cries of dismay, he explained to her that he had no wish other than to avenge Patroklos by killing Hektor. Then Thetis wept.

> She said: 'If that is so, my child, you surely have not long to live; for after Hector's death you are doomed forthwith to die.' 'Then *let* me die forthwith,' Achilles said with passion, 'since I have failed to save my friend from death. He has fallen, far from his motherland, wanting my help in his extremity ...'
>
> Homer *Iliad* 18, 94-100
> (trans. Rieu)

Thetis saw that Achilles had now clearly chosen to have but a brief life and she prepared to help him make it a glorious one.

Being, like most mothers, rather practical, Thetis pointed out to Achilles that he now had no armour and that it was not possible for him to go out and fight naked. She therefore advised him to wait patiently till morning, by which time she would have returned to him bringing a fine new set of armour made by Hephaistos.

Hephaistos, the god of craftsmen, was a most wonderful craftsman himself. He held Thetis in great respect and affection and readily complied with her request to make a new set of armour for Achilles. He laboured until dawn to make it both strong and beautiful.

Athenian red-figure vase painters were also craftsmen and so they had a special sympathy for Hephaistos and his work, but they felt no obligation to glamorise his activities. Thus on a mid-5th century BC vase (Fig. 71), the painter has shown the smith-god as a simple workman, a labourer's cap on his head, his garment tied conveniently around his waist so that his arms can move freely while he works. Greaves and helmet hang already finished on the wall along with various tools, while Hephaistos polishes the shield and Thetis stands by, hand extended, ready to carry the equipment to her son. Homer,

71. Hephaistos makes new armour for Achilles at Thetis' request, Attic red-figure amphora, about 460-450 BC, by the Dutuit Painter, Boston, Museum of Fine Arts (Francis Bartlett Fund).

with poetic licence, described at length the way Hephaistos decorated the shield with images of earth, sky and sea, cities at war and at peace, fields, vineyards and herds. The vase painter, prudently, does not attempt to do likewise.

When Thetis returned to Achilles bringing the divinely made armour, she found him still deep in passionate mourning for his friend. Homer describes him as 'lying prostrate over Patroklos, weeping loud' (*Iliad* 19, 4-5 [trans. Hammond]).

A late 5th century BC vase painter captured the depth of Achilles' emotion, but did so, perhaps surprisingly, by omitting rather than illustrating any dramatic display of feeling (Fig. 72). He has drawn the figures in delicate outline on a white ground. Originally more colours would have been visible. Patroklos has been laid out on a bed which has elaborately turned legs. His name is written above his head which appears to lie peacefully upon the pillow, profile tranquil, eye closed forever in death. Achilles is seated beside him on an elegant chair, his legs crossed, his 'man-slaying' hands lying impotently in his lap. His head is bowed in sorrow. Columns frame the figures (suggesting a grander hut than one might expect for a campaign, but one that is in keeping with the rich furniture). The stillness of the scene conveys the profundity of Achilles' grief as he silently tries to come to terms with the harsh, immutable fact of his friend's death.

Thetis knew full well what the consequences of Achilles' killing Hektor would be, but she knew, too, that the only thing her son now cared about was avenging the murder of his friend. It was, therefore, with immeasurable sadness that she handed over the imperishable armour. Her mood is sensitively caught by a relatively undistinguished vase painter (Fig. 73). The very awkwardness with which he shows her arms wound around her mourning son adds to the poignancy

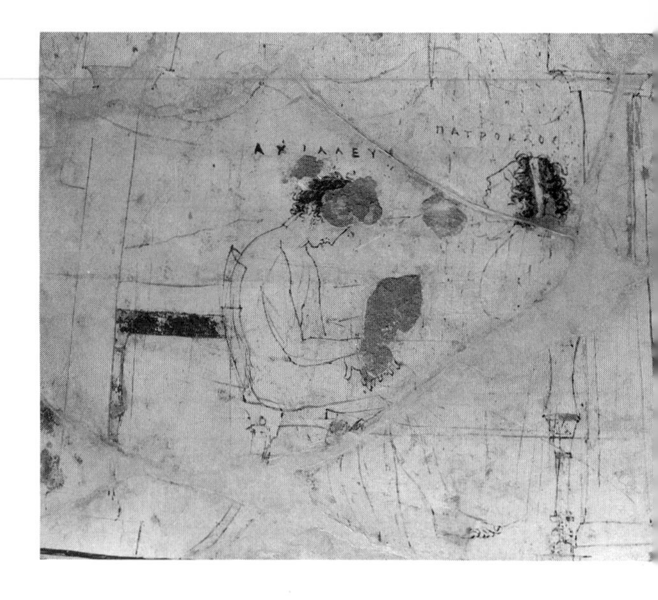

72. Achilles mourning Patroklos (while his mother brings him the new armour), Attic red-figure and white-ground lekythos, about 420 BC, by the Eretria Painter, New York, Metropolitan Museum of Art (Rogers Fund).

of the scene. Achilles is shown muffled in his cloak – the Aeschylean image.

Thetis has been accompanied by two of her sisters; one stands behind Achilles holding the shield. She covers her face with one hand, a wonderfully expressive gesture. The other sister stands to the left, holding spear and helmet.

Homer described Thetis bringing the armour to Achilles all by herself, but Aeschylus, in the second play in his lost trilogy drawn from the story of the *Iliad*, included Thetis' sisters in this scene. The tragedy appears to have been influential.

Armed once more, Achilles was desperately eager to go out and kill Hektor, but before he could do so, certain formalities had to be gone through: a reconciliation with Agamemnon.

Achilles, humbled by suffering, was ready to make the first move. He called the Greeks together and addressed Agamemnon publicly saying:

'Son of Atreus [Agamemnon], could we possibly say that this has proved good for both of us, for you and for me, that the two of us in our passions quarrelled in heart-consuming anger over a girl? I wish that Artemis had killed her with an arrow on board my ships, on that day when I destroyed Lyrnessos, and won her. Then all these many Achaians [Greeks] would not have sunk their teeth in the broad earth, brought down by enemy hands in the time of my great anger ...'

Homer *Iliad* 19, 56-62
(trans. Hammond)

The leaders then became reconciled. Agamemnon restored Briseis, untouched, to Achilles and presented him with many fine gifts by way of compensation, though Achilles no longer cared about such things.

73. Thetis gives Achilles the armour made by Hephaistos, Attic red-figure pelike, about 480-460 BC, by one of the undetermined earlier Mannerists, London, British Museum.

At last Achilles was able to re-enter the fray. Once in battle he laid about him with hideous ferocity, slaying Trojans mercilessly and in great numbers, but for a long time the special object of his fury, Hektor, eluded him.

Finally, however, the two met. All the other Trojans had taken refuge within the walls of Troy, while Hektor, alone, remained outside prepared to confront his great enemy.

Heroic deeds and courageous actions are portrayed over and over in the *Iliad*, but the power of the work resides less in these than in the revelation of the humanity – even the human frailty – of the leading characters. Hektor was no exception. The bulwark of Troy, a man of great bravery and devotion to duty, he was still only a man. When he saw the huge and terrifying Achilles bearing down on him, Hektor's blood ran cold, he began to tremble and his nerve failed: he took to his heels and ran for his life. And after him ran Achilles, swift-footed Achilles. Terror lent speed to the one, fury to the other, and in such a wise they raced around the circuit of the city walls of Troy a full three times. Homer draws on the archetypal image of a nightmare to describe the impasse: a dream in which the pursuer, despite all his efforts, is unable to overtake his quarry and the quarry – for all his desperation – is unable to escape.

Finally Zeus opened out his golden scales.

In the pans he put the two fates of death's long shadow, one for Achilleus and one for Hektor the tamer of horses, and he took the scales in the middle and lifted them up: and Hektor's day of doom sank down, away into Hades, and Phoibos Apollo left him.

Homer *Iliad* 22, 210-213
(trans. Hammond)

74. Achilles (backed up by Athena) attacks Hektor (abandoned by Apollo), Attic red-figure volute krater (neck), about 490-480 BC, by the Berlin Painter, London, British Museum.

Apollo had hoped to help Hektor, but now he was forced to abandon the Trojan hero. Meanwhile Athena, eager to aid the Greeks, rushed to the aid of Achilles. She took on the appearance of Hektor's brother Deiphobos and in this disguise proposed to Hektor that the two of them should make a stand together against Achilles. Hektor was touched by the courage of his brother and his readiness to join him in danger. He stopped running. Hektor and Achilles then faced one another.

Achilles threw his spear first – and missed. But Athena, unseen, returned it to him. Hektor threw next, but his spear rebounded from Achilles' shield. He called to Deiphobos to give him another spear. But Deiphobos was not there. Hektor then realised how he had been deceived and that his death was now upon him. Bravely he drew his sword and attacked, but Achilles charged him with his long spear, aiming carefully at the one spot which was not entirely covered by the bronze armour that had been taken from Patroklos. It was where the collar bones hold the join of neck and shoulders. He struck there and Hektor crashed to the ground. With the last of his failing strength Hektor implored Achilles to give his body back to the Trojans so that he could be properly mourned and buried. But Achilles' hard heart was closed to any appeal from the man who had killed his friend.

The image of Hektor, deceived, abandoned and slain is one of the most touching in the *Iliad* – haunting and terrible. It was a challenge to artists to translate it from words into pictures.

A red-figure vase painter of the early 5th century BC (Fig. 74) has shown Achilles, to the left, charging confidently forward, supported by Athena, who stands encouragingly behind him. Hektor, to the right, falters and falls back. Hektor's arms stretch out helplessly on either side of his exposed, vulnerable body. One hand ineffectually grasps a spear, the other is dragged down by the shield, protection no longer. Apollo, though reluctantly forced to withdraw and leave the hero to his fate, holds his arrow parallel to the failing spear of Hektor, a gesture of support – and a threat, for with his dying breath Hektor reminded Achilles that the day would come when he too would die, slain by the arrow of Paris, guided by the hand of Apollo.

The vase painter has illustrated the sense of the epic, but not the words. Both heroes are nude, though in the poem much is made of the new armour that Achilles sports and the recently acquired armour that Hektor wears. Both heroes hold spears, though the poem makes clear that Hektor's last stand was made with a sword. Hektor falls back, though the poem says he rushed forward. In point after point the image fails to correspond with the words. But such details are trivial. They could be perfectly correctly drawn in an unfeeling picture that moves us not at all. Here they are subordinated to a vision that captures the pathos and the tragedy of the poetic narrative and brings it vividly before our eyes.

Hektor asked for his body to be returned to Troy, but Achilles, his wrath still unappeased, decided to violate it instead. Thus while Hektor's anguished parents continued to watch horrified from the walls of the city, Achilles cut slits behind the tendons of Hektor's ankles and pulled strips of ox-hide through them. He then tied Hektor, feet first, to the back of his chariot and pulled him, head dragging on the ground, back to the Greek camp.

Homer says that Achilles used strips of ox-hide to attach Hektor to his chariot, but a later tradition substituted for them that purple belt which Ajax had given to Hektor at the conclusion of their indecisive single combat.

*

Once Achilles felt that he had avenged his friend's death, he was at last ready to give Patroklos a magnificent funeral. He had a great pyre built and brutally slaughtered twelve Trojan prisoners, four horses and two of Patroklos' own dogs in his honour. Afterwards, to mark the occasion he offered rich prizes to the winners in the contests he proposed to serve as the funeral games for Patroklos.

The principal Greek heroes were eager to compete for the prizes and the glory in chariot-racing, running, archery, boxing and wrestling. Such athletic contests were extremely popular with the later Greeks as well and were often part of their festivals in honour of the gods – the most famous of these being the games at Olympia.

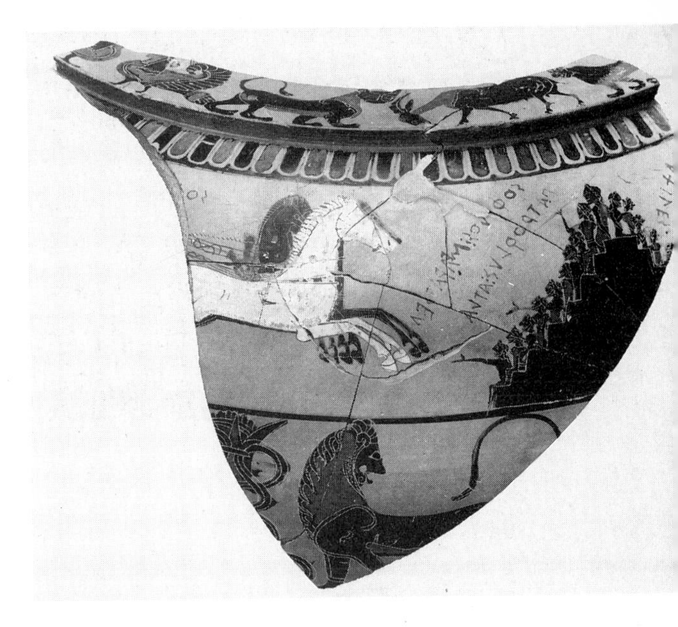

75. Part of the Funeral Games in honour of Patroklos, fragment of a black-figure mixing bowl, about 570 BC, by Sophilos, Athens, National Museum.

Artists in the 6th century BC, therefore, were well acquainted with the excitement that accompanied competitions of this sort and so when the vase painter who signed himself as Sophilos (and had painted Figs. 4-5) illustrated the funeral games for Patroklos, he was as sensitive to the feelings of the spectators as to those of the participants. Only a fragment of his vase has survived (Fig. 75); it shows the leading horses in the winning chariot team galloping home and the grandstand on which the cheering onlookers are seated. The uninhibited liveliness of this small excerpt – surely the bulk of the artist's attention was given to the glorious competitors – gives us immediate access to the artist's own world and insight into his vivid imagining of a legendary scene.

Patroklos' funeral did little to assuage Achilles' grief. Each day Achilles' aching sense of loss for Patroklos vented itself in anger on the lifeless corpse of Hektor. Before dawn Achilles would rise, harness his horses and tie Hektor's body to the chariot. Then he would drive around the tomb of Patroklos, dragging the body of Hektor behind him.

Once again Achilles was behaving in an unseemly manner, for just as before he had carried his resentment of Agamemnon to exaggerated lengths, so now he was taking his vengeance on behalf of Patroklos too far. Decency required that he return the body to Troy for mourning, and his persistent reluctance to do so eventually offended even the gods themselves. Zeus finally summoned Thetis and told her to convey the gods' displeasure to Achilles and to advise him to release the body of Hektor to his father. At the same time, he sent Iris, the messenger goddess, to old Priam to tell him to go fearlessly into the Greek camp and offer ransom to Achilles for his son's body.

In the late 6th century BC, depictions of Achilles' humiliation of the body of his dead enemy became popular among black-figure vase painters. Sometimes many aspects of the story would be compressed within a single frame. One vase (Fig. 76) is so full of action and incident that it is not at all easy to comprehend at first glance. Hektor's grieving parents are shown at the far left. They stand within a portico, which is probably meant to suggest their station on the walls of Troy when they beheld Achilles killing their son and heartlessly dragging his body off the field of battle, his head trailing in the dust. In the centre is shown the chariot, with the body of Hektor tied to the back of it, and Achilles running alongside. Achilles carries a shield and wears a crested helmet. He looks back at the supplicating old people, but rushes forward to leap aboard the speeding chariot. The chariot is driven by a professional charioteer. In the *Iliad* Achilles drove the chariot himself, but the vase painter was used to depicting Homeric battle-scenes in which one man drove the chariot while his partner fought on foot and he has simply transferred the familiar formula to this picture. The winged messenger goddess rushes toward the charioteer on her way to carry her instructions to Priam. At the far right we see the tomb of Patroklos, indicated by a snake, and above it, the ghost of Patroklos (small, winged, and armed) appears in flight.

76. Achilles drags the body of Hektor behind his chariot, Attic black-figure hydria, about 510-500 BC, by one of the painters of the Leagros Group, Boston, Museum of Fine Arts (William Francis Warden Fund).

Several different moments in the story and several different locations are combined in this vigorous image. Hektor's parents are in Troy showing their anguish at the time when Hektor was killed; the tomb of Patroklos was constructed far away, beside the Greek camp, the next day. Several more days had passed before Iris was sent to initiate the sequence of actions that would lead to the return of Hektor's body to his father.

If you know the story, you can unravel the image which gives a précis of events from the death of Hektor to the recovery of his body. The compression of time and space and the abbreviation of the nar-

rative are all legitimate devices used by the vase painter. It is a pity, though, that while his picture is so full of movement physically, emotionally it is hardly moving at all.

In the last book of the *Iliad*, Homer describes how Priam, tactfully escorted by the messenger-god Hermes, goes to Achilles himself and in exchange for a suitably rich ransom recovers the body of his son. When Priam came upon Achilles, he had just

> ... finished his meal and done with eating and drinking: the table was still there beside him. Huge Priam came in unseen, and moving close to him took Achilles' knees in his arms and kissed his hands, those terrible, murderous hands, which had killed many of his sons.
>
> Homer *Iliad* 24, 475-479 (trans. Hammond)

This extraordinarily affecting scene was a challenge to early 5th century BC red-figure vase painters (Fig. 77), but it was not easy for them to give both vivid immediacy and full comprehensibility to so complex a subject.

The fact that Achilles had just finished dining meant to the Greeks of the time that he was still reclining on a couch, and that is how the artist shows him. This part of the scene looks normal enough, but for the fact that Hektor's lifeless body is shown lying beneath the couch. Homer never suggests that Achilles was so crass as to take his pleasure at the table in the presence of the corpse, but the vase painter found it a useful device to indicate that this was no ordinary banquet and an economical way to fill the space under the couch.

77. Priam comes to Achilles to recover the body of Hektor, Attic red-figure cup exterior, first quarter of the 5th century BC, by the 'painter of the fourteenth Brygos', New York, Leon Levy Collection.

Priam is placed in the centre of the scene confronting the two recumbent warriors, Hektor lying dead on the ground and Achilles reclining at the end of his meal. The aged king is sensitively characterised, his body bent beneath the weight of his suffering, his measured pace still preserving some sense of his royal dignity.

Behind Priam, Hermes, the god who has protected the old king on his dangerous journey into the Greek encampment, prepares to take his leave. Behind Achilles, the recently recovered Briseis prepares to crown the hero's head with a wreath. The scene takes place within Achilles' hut, indicated by a column to the left. On the other side of the column stands the first of the procession of Trojans bringing the ransom for the release of Hektor's body.

78. Priam imploring Achilles to return the body of Hektor, silver cup, late 1st century BC – early 1st century AD, Copenhagen, National Museum.

The artist has succeeded well in conveying the grave mood of the encounter in terms that a contemporary viewer would have understood without difficulty.

An even more touching rendering is furnished by the relief decoration on a Roman silver cup (Fig. 78). Achilles is seated here (as Homer must have imagined him to be when he described Priam embracing Achilles' knees, a conventional form of supplication) rather than reclining. Priam wears the Phrygian hat characteristic of Trojans and kneels humbly before Achilles.

This powerfully simple group was probably the invention of a Greek painter of the classical period, perhaps inspired by the last tragedy in Aeschylus' trilogy based on the *Iliad*. The absence of the table mentioned by Homer, which is scrupulously rendered in the vase painting (Fig. 77), and the fact that Achilles sits rather than reclines suggest this.

The image of the old man kneeling before the youth is poignant enough, but the fact that Priam is actually kissing the hand of Achilles makes it almost unbearably moving, for it recalls Priam's words to Achilles in the *Iliad*:

> 'I have brought myself to do a thing that no one else on earth has done – I have raised to my lips the hand of the man who killed my son.'
>
> Homer *Iliad* 24, 505-506 (trans. Rieu)

Achilles released the body to Priam, and with the mourning for Hektor, the *Iliad* closes.

*

The fact that we can still read the Homeric poems (unlike the influential lost Aeschylean tragedies) greatly enriches our appreciation of illustrations from the *Iliad*, for the finest images often resonate with memorable verses. The accessibility of the poem and its vividness may often tempt us to imagine that the ancient artists referred to the text for inspiration. In this we are probably mistaken. It is most likely that an ancient artist would have turned first to a visual model rather than a verbal one in any case. Normally, when depicting a myth he would have relied on earlier depictions, either copying them closely (Figs. 60 and 61), modifying them (Figs. 56-59) or trying to adapt some already existing formula to his current needs (Figs. 63 and 66; 83 and 90), for artists were constantly drawing creatively on the past. Entirely original inventions were rare (Fig. 54).

Artists in antiquity were steeped in mythology; epics and plays were only some of the elements that contributed to the complex store of memories from which an artist would compose his image of a myth. Just because his sources of inspiration were so rich and varied, an ancient artist was usually more inclined to illustrate his own personal vision of a myth as a whole rather than one particular verbal version of it.

Artists occasionally appear to have been remarkably faithful to the Homeric text, but they were often more successful when they did not illustrate it literally or even try to, but rather captured the sense and meaning of an incident, an episode or a whole section of the poem. Illustration, like translation, is never a simple matter of transcription. Words and images can often be complementary, but for all their interdependence each must follow its own rules if it is to speak to the heart.

7

Troy's Doom Draws Nearer

The end of the *Iliad* does not coincide with the end of the Trojan war. The Trojans still had powerful allies who were ready to come to try and save them from the Greek onslaught, and the Greeks still had many reverses to suffer and brave warriors to mourn before they finally took the city.

Shortly after Hektor's body had been returned to Priam and had been properly mourned, the Amazons arrived, eager to fight on the side of the Trojans. The Amazons were a group of legendary warrior women supposed to have lived in northern Asia Minor or in Thrace.

The hero Herakles had been forced to meet the Amazons on their home territory at the time when Laomedon was king in Troy. Herakles had been ordered to fetch the belt of the reigning Amazon queen. Everything went smoothly at first but when suspicions were aroused among some of the Amazons about what exactly Herakles was doing in private conclave with their leader, a nasty brawl developed which soon turned into an all-out battle.

The late 6th century BC red-figure vase painter Euphronios drew a lively picture of Herakles' fight with the Amazons (Fig. 79). Herakles himself, slightly to the left of centre, is immediately recognisable because he is attacking with his club and is wearing the skin of the Nemean lion (p. 47). The lion-skin was often used by artists as an attribute by which to identify the hero; on Fig. 42 he is portrayed wearing the head as a sort of helmet, his face peeping out between its jaws; here he also has the front paws knotted around his neck and the rest of the hide draped over his extended left arm.

Herakles confronts three Amazons, two of whom, marching in step so as to be both decoratively and militarily effective, are equipped like normal heavily-armed warriors (Fig. 79). The third is an archer wearing the trousers that were considered characteristic of Easterners – Paris wears a similar outfit on Fig. 10. Another archer, also dressed in a striped costume, lies fallen at the far left. She is about to be slain by Herakles' companion, Telamon. This formidable pair of Greek heroes has already downed two of their five adversaries, for a shield-wielding Amazon lies at Herakles' feet, her pose almost a mirror-image of Telamon's victim.

It was after having fought the Amazons that Herakles happened to pass by Troy, just in time to rescue Hesione (p. 46). When he was forced to return some time later to punish Laomedon's perfidy and sack the city (pp. 46-8), Telamon was once again by his side.

Although the Amazons had been defeated by Herakles, they had not been entirely eliminated and their daughters turned out just as fierce and bellicose as their mothers had been. Penthesilea, the queen who ruled this younger generation, led her troops with grim determination to fight against the Greeks in defence of

79. Herakles and Telamon fighting Amazons, Attic red-figure volute krater, about 510-500 BC, by Euphronios, Arezzo, Museo Civico.

Priam's Troy.

The Trojans were immensely heartened by the arrival of the Amazons, and their confidence in the effectiveness of their allies at first seemed to be entirely justified. The Amazons fought brilliantly and Penthesilea in particular distinguished herself. Things seemed to be going very much the way of the warrior maiden until she came up against Achilles. There she met her match.

But Achilles' triumph over Penthesilea turned out to be something of a Pyrrhic victory, for, as the hero dealt the fatal blow (or, according to others, as he removed the helmet from the beautiful head of his dead adversary), he was smitten with love for this courageous woman.

The romantic combination of love and death, Achilles being overcome by passion just as its object expires at his hands, presented an exciting challenge to artists.

One of the earliest to tackle the subject, and one of the most successful, was the Athenian black-figure vase painter Exekias, the artist who created such a sensitive image of Ajax and Achilles playing a game (Figs. 54 and 55). On a fine vase (Fig. 80) he illustrated the terrible moment when Achilles plunged his spear into the throat of Penthesilea and at the same time was struck by love for this remarkable opponent who appears to be his female counterpart in both valour and good looks.

The Amazon was apparently trying to escape, but as she fell to one knee, she turned her head back to look up at Achilles. The pupil of her eye has rolled upward and inward indicating the approach of death, and yet she has focused her last glance on her assailant. Achilles looks down into her face. Exekias has succeeded in suggesting that the eyes of slayer and slain have met and that in both their hearts a hopeless love has dawned, a love tragically extinguished the very instant that it is born. Exekias has labelled the figures with neat inscriptions, but the unique situation would have identified them unmistakably in any case.

Other artists tried other devices to show

80. Achilles kills Penthesilea and falls in love with her, Attic black-figure amphora, about 530 BC, by Exekias, London, British Museum.

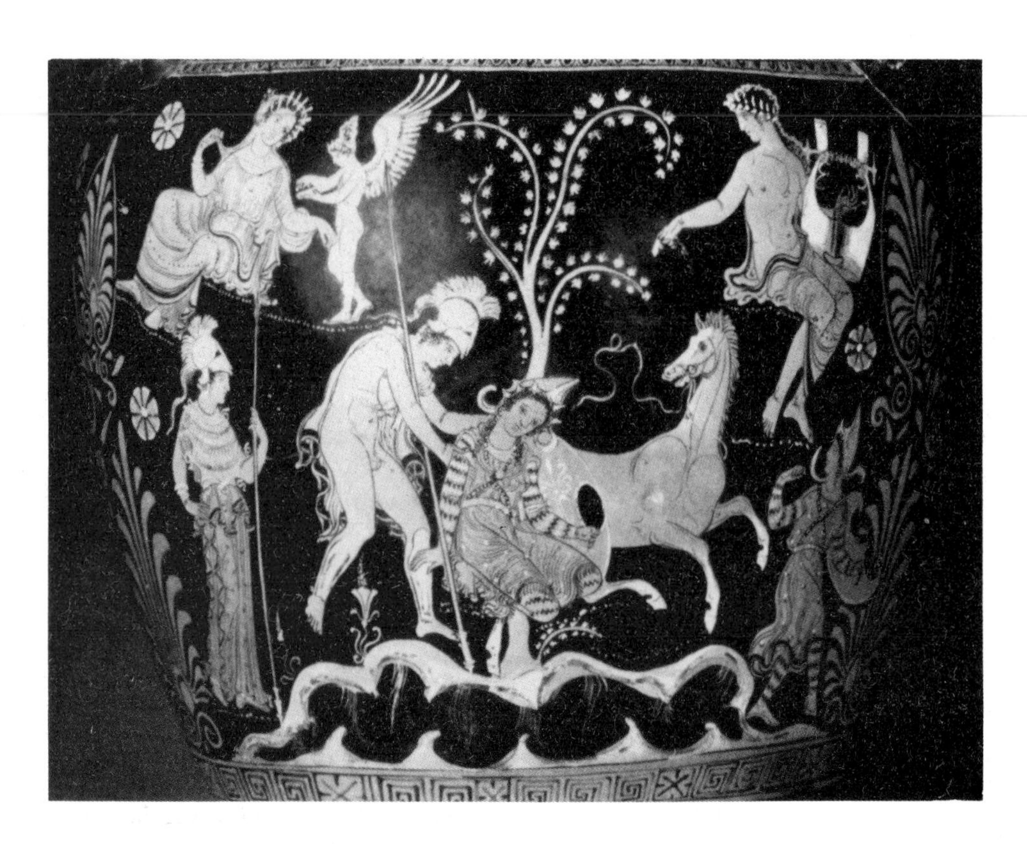

81. Achilles tries to support the stricken Penthesilea in the presence of Athena, Aphrodite, Eros, Apollo, and another Amazon, Apulian red-figure volute krater, about 370-360 BC, by the Lykurgos Painter, Adolphseck, Schloss Fasanerie.

how Achilles' heart was melted by Penthesilea. In the 5th century BC, a painter decorated part of the throne of the great statue of Zeus at Olympia with an image of Achilles supporting the fallen Amazon. The statue (once considered one of the Seven Wonders of the ancient world) no longer exists, but traces of the painter's invention may be reflected in a South Italian vase painting of the 4th century BC (Fig. 81). Penthesilea, wearing what was considered an oriental costume, has fallen from her horse – Amazons, who were originally shown fighting on foot, by the end of the 6th century BC had come to be thought of as particularly fine equestrian warriors. Achilles, having fatally wounded Penthesilea, now comes to her aid and is seen gallantly supporting her shoulders. The surrounding figures serve to gloss the situation. Athena, Achilles' patron, stands behind Achilles, while to the left and above her, Aphrodite is seated attended by Eros. Her presence serves to underline the love motif already signalled by Achilles' solicitude. Opposite Aphrodite, in the upper right-hand corner of the picture, sits Apollo. He, like Aphrodite, is on the side of the Trojans and no friend to Achilles. Aphrodite has afflicted Achilles with a hopeless love. Apollo's vengeance on Achilles is still in the future: he will direct the fatal arrow that finally kills the hero. In the lower right corner, a startled Amazon departs from the scene.

The image of Achilles holding the dead body of his beloved Amazon in his arms continued to intrigue artists. In the 2nd century BC, a free-standing statuary group similar to that of Menelaos with the body of Patroklos (Fig. 69) was created. The

82. Achilles holding the body of Penthesilea in the midst of a heated battle of Greeks and Amazons, Roman sarcophagus, about AD 230-240, Rome, Vatican.

original group is lost, but it was apparently much admired and copied. Some Romans liked to have it adapted for the decoration of their sarcophagi (Fig. 82).

The wealthy Romans who commissioned such expensively carved marble coffins often wanted to be identified with famous figures from mythology as a way of displaying their taste and erudition. Thus the heads of Achilles and Penthesilea (seen in the centre of the panel against a background of frenzied fighting) are not generic types but careful portraits of the dead Roman and his wife. The wife was obviously a lady of fashion, and so, despite her Amazonian disguise, she is shown as if fresh from the beauty salon wearing the most up-to-date contemporary hair style.

Battles of Greeks and Amazons were very popular, particularly among Athenian black-figure vase painters. They illustrated Herakles' fight with the Amazons most often, but they also represented the Amazons who fought beside the Trojans and other legendary conflicts in which the Amazons were involved. Many incidents recur repeatedly on different vases, but one vase is unusual in showing a Greek warrior carrying the body of an Amazon out of the fray as if she were an ally (Fig. 83). No names are inscribed beside the figures, but it seems likely that the artist here had in mind Achilles' infatuation with Penthesilea and that he employed a composition usually reserved for representations of a warrior rescuing the body of a cherished comrade (see Figs. 90 and 91) in order to convey it.

*

83. Achilles carries the dead Penthesilea out of battle, Attic black-figure hydria, about 510-500 BC, by one of the painters of the Leagros Group, London, British Museum.

84. Hermes weighing the destinies of Memnon and Achilles in the presence of their anxious mothers, Eos and Thetis, Attic red-figure cup, about 450 BC, Paris, Louvre.

The hopes of the Trojans, which had been sadly dashed with the defeat of Penthesilea and her Amazons, rose again when Memnon appeared with fresh troops, ready to fight on their side. Memnon, the son of Eos and the Trojan Tithonos (p. 44), was king of the Ethiopians. His sympathies naturally lay with the Trojans and he and his people were ready to take up arms against the invading Greeks.

Like Penthesilea, Memnon was, at first, wonderfully successful, but eventually, like Penthesilea, he met his match in Achilles.

Both Memnon and Achilles were sons of goddesses and so the stakes in this conflict, not only on earth but also on Olympus, were unusually high. Homer says that when Hektor and Achilles were about to clash in their fateful conflict, Zeus held up his golden scales and weighed the fates of the two contending heroes. Tradition also associates the idea of weighing the destinies of two heroes with this fight between Memnon and Achilles, and in art the image appears much more often in this context.

Normally Hermes, the servant of Zeus, is shown holding the scales in which the fates of the two heroes are weighed (Fig. 84). Sometimes the two warriors are shown actually fighting, while their anxious mothers await the outcome of the weighing, but often, as on this cup exterior, attention is focused on the mothers, both of whom have made pleas for the lives of their beloved sons.

The destinies of the two heroes are represented as miniature warriors, one in each pan of the scales. The two distracted mothers rush off in opposite directions – presumably to inform their sons, who are engaged in fighting on the other side of the cup. Hermes gestures toward Thetis, and she turns her head back to look at him. Her son is destined to triumph in this conflict. Thetis is shown as wingless; her rival, Eos, is shown, as so often, winged (cf. Figs. 34, 35, 86 and 87).

The mothers' involvement in their sons' struggles fascinated vase painters. Sometimes they were careful to distinguish the winged Eos from the wingless Thetis, as in Fig. 84, but at other times a sense of the equal intensity of their passionate maternal feelings overwhelmed any superficial distinction between them. Thus on one vase (Fig. 85) Thetis holds out anxious hands toward Achilles (on the left) who rushes at Memnon with his spear poised for action. Memnon, meanwhile, seen in back view, has drawn his sword. The short sword, still held behind the hero, has little chance against the long spear already advanced for action. Eos, on the far right, holds her hand to her head, anticipating the dreadful outcome. All the figures are labelled with inscriptions, but for those who know that

85. Achilles attacking Memnon, while Thetis and Eos watch, Attic red-figure volute krater (neck), about 490 BC, by the Berlin Painter (the other side of Fig. 74), London, British Museum.

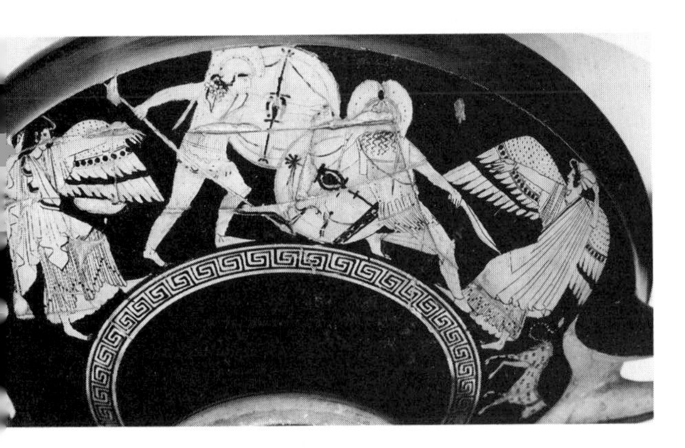

86. Achilles attacking Memnon, while Thetis and Eos watch, Attic red-figure cup, 490-480 BC, by the Castelgiorgio Painter, London, British Museum.

this is the only mythical occasion on which two divine mothers had to witness a duel between their two mortal sons, the scene would be immediately recognisable even without such aids.

Another vase painter (Fig. 86) has illustrated a slightly later moment in the same conflict. Memnon, shown in back view on the right, has already fallen to Achilles' onslaught. The mothers flank the combatants. In this case the feeling for the parallelism of the plight of the two divine parents may actually have gone a little too far. It has not only obliterated the differences in their appearance – for here they are both shown winged – but has also made them display identical emotional reactions. The poses of the two goddesses are virtual mirror-images of one another. Each extends one hand toward the centre and grasps her head with the other. The artist's concern to create a balanced picture has overwhelmed his sensitivity to the story that he is telling, for only one of the mothers is doomed to suffer on her son's behalf.

These examples show how variously artists can respond to the same task. In some instances they keep clearly in mind that Eos is the goddess of dawn and ought normally to be shown with wings, while Thetis, a sea goddess, has no use for such appendages. At other times, whether for the sake of compositional balance or in order to illustrate a balance in emotional weight, the two goddesses are made into symmetrical counterparts of one another, either both winged (Fig. 86) or both wingless (Fig. 85).

The death of Memnon was a terrible shock to Eos. In her grief she was even ready to abandon her duty of bringing light to the world. An early 5th century BC red-figure vase painter has drawn a tender picture of the eternally youthful goddess sorrowfully lifting the body of her dead son (Fig. 87). Restrained and yet poignant, the simple drawing on the interior of a cup foreshadows many later images of the Virgin Mary mourning the dead Christ, the Pietà of Christian iconography.

*

87. Eos with the body of Memnon, Attic red-figure cup interior, about 490 BC, by Douris, Paris, Louvre.

88. Apollo directs the fatal arrow shot by Paris at Achilles, Attic red-figure pelike, about 460 BC, by the Niobid Painter, Bochum, Antikenmuseum, Ruhr-Universität.

Achilles had proved himself a mighty warrior, but it was fated that he should die like many another. Although the way he died was generally agreed, there were several traditions as to exactly where he was killed. According to one version, Achilles was slain outside Troy at the Skaian gate, while according to another he was lured inside the city to the temple of Apollo. He went there because of the love he had conceived for the Trojan princess Polyxena. He had first caught a glimpse of her either when she was accompanying her brother Troilos, whom Achilles ambushed at the fountain house (see Figs. 49, 50, 51 and 53) or when she stood upon the walls and offered to contribute to the ransom for the recovery of her brother Hektor's body. In any case, Achilles fell so much in love with her and so passionately desired her that he was even willing to enter a temple of Apollo in order to obtain her. A temple of Apollo was a dangerous place for him, for he had grievously insulted the god when he had slain Troilos at his shrine (p. 58).

Wherever the incident may have occurred, most traditions agreed that Paris shot the fatal arrow and that Apollo directed it to the fatal place. A rather undramatic but explicit red-figure vase painting makes this perfectly clear (Fig. 88). Paris stands at the left with drawn bow. Apollo stands in the centre unobtrusively redirecting the course of the arrow, which now plunges abruptly downward. It is headed for Achilles' heel, long considered his only vulnerable point. As we have seen, later tradition accounted for this anatomical peculiarity by explaining that Thetis had held Achilles by the heel (or ankle) when she dipped him in the Styx (see Figs. 14 and 15) so that this area alone remained untouched by the magic of the waters.

An earlier black-figure vase painter prominently displays the arrow in dead Achilles' ankle, though he also shows another arrow piercing Achilles' side (Fig. 89). Paris can be seen sneaking away at the far right, bow stretched, perhaps preparing to shoot again. Ajax stands boldly over the body of Achilles, defending it, while Athena, behind him, watches.

In the *Iliad*, Ajax was considered second only to Achilles as a warrior. In time he became increasingly closely related to Achilles not only in fighting ability, but also in lineage. Homer knew that Achilles' father was Peleus and that Ajax's father was Telamon, that very Telamon who had sacked Troy by the side

89. The death of Achilles, Chalcidian black-figure amphora, about 550-540 BC, lost.

90. Ajax carrying the body of Achilles, Attic black-figure decoration on the handle of the François vase (see Fig. 51), about 570 BC, by Kleitias, Florence, Museo Archeologico.

of Herakles a generation before. A post-Homeric verbal tradition made Peleus and Telamon brothers, so that Achilles and Ajax became cousins, and this may have stimulated the post-Homeric visual tradition that brought the two heroes together in their absorption in playing a game (see Figs. 54-59). Not surprisingly, most post-Homeric traditions also agreed that it was Ajax, seen defending the body of Achilles on Fig. 89, who eventually carried the hero's corpse away from the battlefield and back to the camp.

A small drawing on the handle of a vase by Kleitias illustrates this with eloquent simplicity (Fig. 90). Ajax is depicted in the bent-knee pose that conventionally indicates running, but here it may also suggest that the hero is solemnly rising as he prepares to carry the dead weight of his friend away from the field of battle. His head and torso are upright, his limbs extended or bent at right angles. The placement of virtually all parts of his body along either verticals or horizontals produces a compositional stability that powerfully contributes to the sombre mood of tragedy.

The huge body of Achilles, slung over Ajax's shoulders, occupies most of the available space on either side of him. Achilles' well-muscled legs, their swiftness stilled forever, dominate the left side of the picture; the drooping lifeless hair, paralleled by the helplessly dangling fingers of the once 'man-slaying hands' closes the right side. Sensitive incision contrasts the serious, grave, round eye of Ajax with the closed, unseeing eye of Achilles. The heroes' names are written beside them, discreetly filling the otherwise blank corners and making clear that these are no ordinary warriors.

The visual formula used here was clearly much appreciated and was employed, though rather less subtly, by later artists. One example (Fig. 91) shows how it was adapted to fit into the centre of a cup. The ambiguity between running and rising has been sacrificed in the interest of showing Ajax running rapidly, his lower leg bent upwards at a sharp angle to his thigh. Achilles' hanging hair seems less pathetically limp, but it is nicely balanced by his pointed toes; his slightly flexed arm, however, no longer justified by Ajax's hold upon it, has lost the suggestion of a lifeless body. The

91. Ajax carrying the body of Achilles, Attic black-figure cup interior, about 550 BC, by the Phrynos Painter, Rome, Vatican.

image is a vigorous one, well designed, along with the inscriptions, to fill the circular space, but it has neither the dignity nor the pathos of the earlier version (Fig. 90).

The early 6th century BC visual formula for showing Ajax carrying the body of Achilles could be adapted not only to fill a circle, but also to illustrate another subject. Thus Achilles carrying the body of Penthesilea on Fig. 83, with the limply hanging hands, hair and toes, shows its dependence on the earlier type.

Artists were always eager to draw on successful formulae and to adapt them wherever they might serve effectively.

*

When Achilles had set off for the war, he had been instructed to become the foremost as 'a speaker of words and a doer of deeds', that is, wise in counsel and brave in battle. So well had he accomplished these goals that his loss was deeply mourned.

In the end, however, Achilles' body, like that of most other heroes who died at Troy, was burned on a pyre. Then, as the Roman poet Ovid observed,

> he was reduced to ashes, and of the great Achilles there remained only a little handful, scarcely enough to fill an urn ...
> Ovid *Metamorphoses* 12, 615-616
> (trans. Innes)

But the armour of Achilles, armour of unparalleled magnificence, made by the smith-god Hephaistos himself, was preserved. Thetis, Achilles' mother, now offered this priceless armour to 'the best of the Greeks'.

Only two heroes dared to step forward to claim it: Ajax, well known to Homer as 'second only to Achilles,' and Odysseus. Neither could pretend to have fulfilled their manhood as completely as Achilles. Ajax was unquestionably a great 'doer of deeds', but without any pronounced gifts as a speaker; by contrast, Odysseus was immensely clever in speech, but not as valiant a fighter. Neither one could entirely fill the armour of Achilles.

Vase painters, who appreciated the tempestuous character of heroes, did not hesitate to show them quarrelling, about to come to blows. On Fig. 92 the artist has clearly indicated the cause of the altercation. The arms of Achilles (helmet, shield, greaves and cuirass) lie on the ground in the centre. A dignified man with a sceptre, presumably the commander-in-chief, Agamemnon, stands behind them. Ajax, just to the left, has advanced to claim them as his own, when he notices the approach of the unexpected challenger, Odysseus. Angry and insulted, he has drawn his sword on the impudent interloper. Friends grasp his arm and try to restrain him. To the right, Odysseus has stepped forward, about to make his claim. Observing Ajax's violent response, he starts to draw his sword to defend himself, while friends on his side (the upper parts of their bodies lost) also try to avert any bloodshed.

The rich implications of the contest for the arms of Achilles were, however, better realised in literature. From the time of Aeschylus (who dramatised this conflict in his lost tragedy *The Judgement of Arms*) the dispute could be envisioned in terms of a display of rival speeches. Such debates, even when cast in the mythological past, could embody passionately held feelings, though they could also develop into routine declamatory exercises.

In a contest of words, Odysseus' victory was a foregone conclusion, but his tactics might, according to one's point of view, be considered either laudable or despicable. Opinions polarised around the two claimants. Supporters of Odysseus saw a contest of brains versus brawn, intelligence outshining brute force, while the admirers of Ajax were alarmed that noble simplicity might be overcome by cunning falsehood.

By the time Ovid composed rival

92. Ajax and Odysseus quarrelling over the arms of Achilles, Attic red-figure cup exterior, about 500-480 BC, by Douris, Vienna, Kunsthistorisches Museum.

speeches for the two heroes in the 1st century BC/AD, he was hardly doing something new; nevertheless, the arguments he so cleverly presents are worth looking at more closely:

Ajax begins. He first cites his martial valour (as it had been portrayed by Homer) and then turns to his noble lineage, recalling that his father was Telamon, who conquered Troy with Herakles, and reminds the Greeks that he himself was Achilles' cousin. He accuses Odysseus of cowardice, of acting effectively only when accompanied by Diomedes, and of having injured the Greek cause by recommending that Philoktetes be abandoned on Lemnos (p. 54). Nor does he fail to contrast his own forthright valour with Odysseus' timidity and preference for scheming rather than action. Finally he concludes:

> 'But what is the use of talking? Let us once and for all be seen in action. Throw the arms of our hero into the midst of the enemy's ranks. Bid us seek them there, and deck the one who brings them back with the weapons he has recovered.'
>
> Ovid *Metamorphoses* 13, 120-123 (trans. Innes)

The audience was, naturally, much impressed. But then Odysseus began to speak, and he spoke in a most engaging manner. According to Ovid:

> 'If my wishes and yours had prevailed, O Greeks,' he said, 'there would be no vexed question of an heir, to cause such strife. You, Achilles, would still have your own arms, and we should still have you. But, my friends, since the cruel fates have denied us our hero,' and he pretended to brush the tears from his eyes with his hand – 'who better should succeed the great Achilles than the man through whom Achilles took his place among the Greeks? I only ask you not to

93. The Greeks deciding by vote whether the arms of Achilles should go to Ajax or Odysseus, Attic red-figure cup exterior by Douris, the other side of Fig. 92.

favour my opponent because he appears to be a blunt fellow – as indeed he is – or be prejudiced against me because of my cleverness which has always been used to your advantage. Do not let this eloquence of mine, if indeed I have any, give rise to ill-feeling. It pleads now for its master, but has often been used on your behalf. Each man must employ the talents that he has.'

Ovid *Metamorphoses* 13, 128-138
(trans. Innes)

Odysseus then goes on to defend himself brilliantly. He reminds the Greeks that it was due to his clever ruse that Achilles was discovered among the daughters of Lykomedes and persuaded to come to Troy in the first place (p. 29). He cites his other services to the Greeks, such as his ingenuity in luring Iphigeneia to Aulis and persuading her father to sacrifice her, and he challenges the inarticulate Ajax to induce the angry and resentful Philoktetes to forgive the Greeks and come to fight with them at Troy (as this had recently been found to be a necessary condition for the fall of the city). One way and another, he refutes Ajax's charges and is awarded the arms.

Tradition is unanimous that Odysseus won the contest, though there were many different ideas as to how the decision was reached. Athenian vase painters seem to have assumed that the method used was a vote, the sort of democratic method that would have been employed in their own city in their own time. The vote is depicted on the outside of a cup (Fig. 93 – on the side opposite Fig. 92, which shows the quarrel over the arms). Athena stands behind the low table on which the voting pebbles are placed. Anyone knowing how much she favoured Odysseus could guess the outcome. Ajax, standing at the far right, head veiled, turns away in despair. He has guessed. Odysseus stands at the far left; he raises his hands in delight as the pebbles build up on his side.

Odysseus had many admirers in antiquity, but sympathy for Ajax was not lacking. Two famous painters in the late 5th century BC, Timanthes and Parrhasios, competed in a portrayal of Ajax and the award of the arms. When the prize went to Timanthes, Parrhasios wittily remarked that 'in the name of the hero he was grieved at being worsted a second time by an unworthy rival' (Pliny the Elder *Natural History* 35, 72 [trans. Jex-Blake]).

The blow to Ajax's pride when the arms of Achilles were denied him was one from which he could never recover. There now seemed to be only two alternatives left for him: revenge or death.

According to the tradition drawn upon by Sophokles in his tragedy *Ajax*, Ajax first tried his hand at revenge. Sophokles, like Ovid, suggests that the Greek generals gave the decision about the arms of Achilles and it was therefore from them that Ajax sought satisfaction for his wrongs. Smarting from their lack of appreciation of what he had done in fighting for them, Ajax resolved that he would kill them all. He set out with this intention, when the vigilant Athena, fearing for her protégés, made him go mad. Thus Ajax was diverted from the tents of the generals and strayed off instead among the flocks and herds that were kept to supply the troops. He then began to massacre the beasts under the illusion that they were the Greek chiefs.

When he came to his senses, his humiliation was complete. Whether he was ashamed to have been caught trying to murder his erstwhile allies or whether he was ashamed because he had failed in this intention, there was nothing left for him but to put a dignified end to himself.

The unhappy fate of Ajax, a great man who had suffered greatly, inspired Exekias. He drew a wonderfully poignant picture of Ajax preparing for his suicide (Fig. 94).

The hero has retired to a secluded place, its isolation indicated by the lonely palm tree. He has set his famous shield to one side and now he is busy planting his sword in the ground, preparatory to falling upon it. There is little action here, but intense, solemn concentration. The wrinkled brow, the bowed head, the long delicate fingers patting down the earth with infinite care – all these details so meticulously thought out and so precisely executed show Exekias' heartfelt sensitivity to the plight of the disgraced hero. Ajax is punctilious here as never before. He does not want his suicide to misfire and turn into some ludicrous parody as his attempt to kill the Greek leaders had. The unfitting end of a heroic life could hardly be expressed more tragically.

Exekias' vision was personal and original. Almost a century later Sophokles captured something of the same feeling for a great man so cruelly robbed of dignity, yet striving to make a decent end for himself, in his tragedy *Ajax*. But most

94. Ajax prepares to commit suicide, Attic black-figure amphora, about 540 BC, by Exekias, Boulogne-sur-Mer, Musée des Beaux-Arts et d'Archéologie.

 Fig. 32

95. Ajax having committed suicide (the Greek generals Nestor, Phoinix, Agamemnon, Odysseus, Diomedes, Teukros and Ajax son of Oileus discover the body), Corinthian black-figure cup, about 580 BC, by the Cavalcade Painter, Basel, Antikenmuseum (loan).

artists had a more straightforward approach: they simply showed the climactic moment when Ajax was discovered, having fallen on his sword, and they made no bones about making clear exactly where the sword entered and where it left the body of the unfortunate hero (Fig. 95).

The sword itself was, of course, no ordinary weapon, for this was the sword that Hektor had given Ajax when the two parted after their inconclusive single combat (see Fig. 65). In Hektor's hands the sword could inflict no injury on Ajax, but in his own it proved fatal.

There were those, however, who believed that Ajax could not even commit suicide without encountering some complication or humiliation. One tradition maintained that when Ajax fell upon his sword, he found to his dismay that nothing happened. Repeated attempts to kill himself with increasing vigour only led to the result that the sword itself bent like a bow – but it could not penetrate the skin. The reason for this was that Ajax had been made almost entirely invulnerable when he was a baby. According to this story, when Ajax was still an infant, Herakles visited his old friend Telamon, Ajax's father, to congratulate him on the birth of his son. In taking the child in his arms, he enfolded the baby in the skin of the Nemean lion, which he was wearing. Everywhere the garment touched the infant, the skin of the baby became as invulnerable as the skin of the lion (p. 47). Only a small area around the armpit was not touched, because Herakles' quiver got in the way. Homer gives no hint of the invulnerability of Ajax, but Aeschylus, in his lost tragedy on the humiliating end of the hero, explained that Ajax was finally able to do away with himself only when a helpful spirit indicated to him the one spot where the sword could penetrate.

Pindar may have had this story in mind when he described Herakles coming to Telamon to summon him to the war against Troy, pouring out a libation and making the prayer:

> 'If ever, O father Zeus, thou hast heard my prayer with willing heart, now, even now, with strong entreaty I pray thee to bring to perfection for Telamon a brave son ... I pray thee to make him as hardy in frame as this hide that is wrapped around me, hide of the beast whom, as the very first of my labours, I slew that day in Nemea; and may he have courage to match.'
>
> Pindar *Isthmian Ode* 6, 44-49
> (trans. Sandys)

It was with such high hopes that the career of Ajax was begun, only to end, miserably, in solitude and disgrace.

8

The Fall of Troy

Nine long years were destined to pass, the Greeks knew, before Troy would fall to them. But as the tenth year of the war dragged on, the city still held out.

Fighting alone, it seemed, could never bring Troy down. Other conditions had also to be met; the city was hedged about with protective talismans. When the siege was still in its infancy the Greeks had learned of one of them: that Troy would be impregnable if Priam's young son Troilos reached the age of 20. Achilles had ensured that this obstacle was removed by killing the boy (Figs. 49-51). But in the course of the tenth year of the war Achilles himself died, and so too did the mighty Ajax. The Greeks began to despair.

And then, luckily, they got hold of some vital information: Troy *could* be taken, but only with the aid of the son of Achilles and the bow of Herakles.

The son of Achilles, Neoptolemos by name, had been fathered on the island of Skyros (p. 29) and was now growing into a young man. Greek emissaries set off at once to summon him. Neoptolemos' mother was reluctant to let him go, for she feared that she would lose her son in the same way that she had lost her husband, but the youth himself was eager to follow in his father's footsteps. The task of bringing Neoptolemos to Troy was, therefore, easily accomplished. Once the boy arrived, Odysseus promptly turned over to him his father's glorious armour – that very armour of Achilles which had caused such dissension in the Greek camp and which had finally led to the suicide of Ajax.

Achilles' celebrated armour had been made by no less a smith than the god Hephaistos himself (Fig. 71) and was unparalleled in both workmanship and prestige. Its significance was well appreciated by the Athenian red-figure vase painter, Douris, who chose the arms of Achilles as the unifying theme for his decoration of an elegant cup. Three areas of the cup were available for decoration, the two sides between the handles on the exterior and the centre of the bowl on the interior. Douris, therefore, divided the story of the arms of Achilles into three episodes. He painted one side of the exterior with the scene of the dispute between Odysseus and Ajax (Fig. 92) and the other side with a picture of the vote to decide between the two contenders (Fig. 93). He completed the story on the interior of the cup by showing Odysseus delivering the arms to Neoptolemos (Fig. 96).

The vertical axis of the circle is occupied by the helmet, cuirass and greaves, placed one above the other in an anthropomorphically suggestive arrangement, as if something of the aura of a ghostly warrior were still hovering about them. The young, beardless Neoptolemos stands to the left. He holds the helmet in his left hand and with his right grasps the cuirass which Odysseus is proffering him. Odysseus, dignified and bearded, stands

96. Neoptolemus receives the arms of Achilles from Odysseus, Attic red-figure cup interior by Douris (of which the exterior is shown in Figs. 92 and 93).

to the right, the elaborately decorated shield still on his arm, the spear in his hand.

The scene is serious and solemn. Greek heroes who were the sons of famous fathers felt the weight of expectation that rested heavily upon them. Ajax was ashamed of his disgrace and preferred suicide to facing a father who had succeeded in capturing Troy where he had failed. Neoptolemos had never met his father, but he was deeply impressed by his great reputation. This was, indeed, a challenge to live up to. Accepting the arms of Achilles meant accepting the responsibility. The thoughtful youth appreciated this fact.

Having successfully secured the aid of the son of Achilles, the Greeks now had to consider how they could obtain the bow of Herakles. This bow had been given to Philoktetes by Herakles upon his death (Fig. 45). Philoktetes himself had brought it with him when he had joined the expedition to Troy, but both he and it had been abandoned years before on the island of Lemnos when the consequences of a snake's bite had made Philoktetes' presence intolerable (Fig. 48). Time had not cured Philoktetes' wound, nor had isolation improved his disposition. Lonely and resentful, he eked out a living shooting birds and small game with Herakles' powerful weapons and suffering ghastly bouts of pain. As he nursed his incurable wound, he also nursed his hatred of the Greek leaders who had abandoned him to such a miserable fate (Fig. 97).

According to tradition, this unhappy story had a happy ending: in the tenth year of the war Philoktetes was retrieved from his island exile and brought to Troy where his wound was healed and his valour finally displayed and amply acknowledged.

This simple resolution of an awkward situation satisfied some poets, but not the great Athenian tragedians of the 5th century BC. They pondered the difficulties involved in overcoming the accumulated hostility of the long-neglected hero and reconciling him with the men he blamed for his prolonged period of suffering. Aeschylus, Sophokles and Euripides all composed tragedies dealing with the problem of how Philoktetes was persuaded to come to Troy to help the Greeks. Only traces remain of how Aeschylus and Euripides treated the story, but Sophokles' *Philoktetes* survives in its entirety.

Sophokles created a thoroughly plausible character for Philoktetes, one who had so long brooded on his sufferings and so nourished his resentment that neither cure nor glory could tempt him into forgiving those he considered responsible for his misery. Something of that character is caught in a late 5th century BC vase painting which shows Philoktetes in

97. Philoktetes on Lemnos, Attic red-figure lekythos, about 430 BC, by a painter near the Eretria Painter, New York, Metropolitan Museum (Fletcher Fund).

his enforced isolation sitting under a lonely tree, his injured foot resting on a support, the treasured bow on the ground beside him (Fig. 97). The hero is completely turned in on himself, a psychological state emphasised by the setting, the bough of the tree bending in front of his face, cutting him off from outside communication.

In Sophokles' tragedy, *Philoktetes*, the wily Odysseus sailed to Lemnos accompanied by the idealistic son of Achilles to fetch Philoktetes. By means of deception, Neoptolemos was able to get hold of the bow of Herakles. Odysseus declared that this was sufficient and that if Philoktetes himself declined to come, he was ready just to take the bow and abandon the miserable and unarmed Philoktetes to his fate. But before the Greeks could sail away, the noble Neoptolemos had a change of heart. He had deplored the deception that Odysseus had persuaded him to practise and, touched by Philoktetes' plight, in a surprise move, he returned his precious weapon to the hero. The embittered Philoktetes had remained uncompromisingly committed to his opposition to the Greeks and the Greek cause throughout, regardless of how hopeless his own position became. Nothing, it seemed, could deflect him from his hatred.

Tradition required that Philoktetes go to Troy, but Sophokles had drawn the character of Philoktetes so firmly and made it so coherent and convincing that it seemed impossible for either the cunning Odysseus or the noble Neoptolemos to persuade – or even to coerce – the hero to do so. In the end Sophokles had to resort to a *deus ex machina*, that is, he closed the play by making Herakles, now a god, order Philoktetes to swallow his resentment and go to Troy.

Sophokles' fascinating tragedy demonstrates how a poet could, by introducing original characterisations and unexpected reversals, bring fresh excitement and suspense to a familiar tale.

Once Philoktetes arrived at Troy, his wound was healed by one of the camp doctors, as had been foretold, and he quickly won glory for the Greeks and for himself.

Since he was the possessor of the celebrated bow of Herakles, Philoktetes naturally distinguished himself as an archer, and it was not long before his skill was pitted against the best of the Trojan archers: Paris.

Paris was a fine bowman, highly successful on his own (Fig. 89), irresistible when aided by a god (Fig. 88). It was he who had started the war by stealing Helen (Figs. 11, 12 and 13) and it was he who had enraged the Greeks by killing Achilles. Now, at last, he had met his match. And so Paris fell to Philoktetes, and the final chapter of the Trojan war began.

*

When the arms of Achilles were awarded to Odysseus, it was on the basis of the argument that battles may be won by brawn but wars are only won by brains. Ajax may have excelled in the former; but unquestionably it was Odysseus who excelled in the latter. Agamemnon defended the decision (according to Sophokles in his tragedy *Ajax*) by pointing out:

> '... It's not a man's great frame
> Or breadth of shoulders makes his
> manhood count:
> A man of sense has always the
> advantage.
> A very little whip can serve to guide
> A hulking ox straight forward on his
> road.'
>
> Sophokles *Ajax* 1250-1254
> (trans. Moore)

Odysseus now had to prove that the decision had been the correct one. He needed an idea – and a good one.

Inspired by Athena, he devised the following scheme: he had the craftsman Epeios build a huge hollow wooden horse. The horse was inscribed with the words: 'For their return home, the Greeks dedicate this thank-offering to Athena.' It was left standing in the Trojan plain.

Meanwhile the Greeks burned their camp and sailed away. Virgil, in the *Aeneid*, tells the story of what happened next from the Trojans' point of view:

> ... So all the land of Troy relaxed after its years of unhappiness. We flung the gates open and we enjoyed going to look at the unoccupied, deserted space along the shore where the Greek camp had been. ... Some of us looked in awed wonder at that massive horse, the gift for Minerva [Athena] ... Thymoetes, perhaps out of treason or perhaps because Troy's fate was already fixed, was first to make a proposal: we should tow the horse inside the city walls and leave it standing on our citadel. But others ... advised us to destroy it by casting it down into the sea or by setting fire to it and burning it; or else to pierce it and tear open the hidden lair within. The rest were divided in keen support of one proposal or the other.
>
> Virgil *Aeneid* 2, 26-39
> (trans. Jackson Knight)

At this point a new factor emerged. Some shepherds had captured what appeared to be a badly frightened Greek. His name was Sinon. The story he told was that the Greeks, before departing for home, had been advised to propitiate the gods with a human sacrifice. This was to ensure a good wind to take them to Greece, just as the sacrifice of Iphigeneia had procured them a good wind when they set out for Troy. Sinon had been selected to be the victim, but he had managed to escape. After a while the Greeks had given up searching for him and had departed.

When asked about the wooden horse, Sinon explained that it had been built to placate Athena. It had been constructed on such a large scale in order to prevent the Trojans from bringing it into their city, for were the horse to be sheltered within the citadel, not only would the city be protected, but the Trojans would have the power to attack the Greeks.

Many Trojans began to think that it might well be worth while enlarging their gates or even tearing down their walls in order to bring this huge talisman over to their side. But not all of them were convinced. The priest Laocoon, in particular, objected. From the first he had been suspicious. According to Virgil, he had warned the Trojans:

> '... Do you really believe that your enemies have sailed away? Do you think that a Greek could offer a gift without treachery in it? ... Either some of their men have been shut inside this timberwork and are now hiding in it, or the horse itself is a machine for overcoming our walls ... Trojans, never trust that horse. Whatever it proves to be, I still fear the Greeks, even when they offer

gifts.' As he spoke, he powerfully heaved a great spear at the horse's side, into the firm timber-work of its rounded belly, and there it stood, quivering. At the impact, the echoing spaces of the cavernous womb growled and rang; and if the destined will of Heaven had not been set against us, and our own reason deranged, Laocoon had surely driven home a thrust till the iron tore open the Greek lair.

Virgil *Aeneid* 2, 43-55
(trans. Jackson Knight)

Now, as the Trojans pondered what they should do about the horse, Laocoon was preparing to make a sacrifice to the gods. Suddenly a pair of monstrous snakes emerged from the sea and attacked Laocoon and his two sons. A famous statuary group, much appreciated by the Romans, depicted this gruesome scene by means of some extraordinarily bold stone-carving (Fig. 98). Laocoon's mighty body is shown writhing within the coils of the encircling snakes. His anguished face starkly reveals his torment; his brows are drawn diagonally upward toward the bridge of his nose in a reflex response to pain, while his mouth opens to emit a groan. Laocoon's younger son, to the left, droops, apparently having succumbed to the reptilian attack unlike his older brother, on the right, who still anxiously attempts to disentangle himself from the monsters' grip. The snakes weave in and out, knotting the three figures together in horrible, ever contracting, inescapable bonds.

98. Laocoon and his two sons attacked by snakes, probably a Roman marble copy made after an original created during the Hellenistic period, Rome, Vatican.

Traditions vary as to exactly what offence Laocoon had committed to warrant this punishment and as to who of the three victims attacked by the snakes were killed, but all agree that the terrifying assault was manifestly a sign of divine intervention. The Trojans drew their own conclusions, as Virgil recounts:

Men said that Laocoon had deserved to pay for his wickedness in damaging the sacred woodwork with his lance, when he had made his sinful cast at the horse's side. All were loud in their desire for the horse to be towed to its rightful place ...

We cut through our walls and threw our defences open. All set to work with zest. Rollers for smooth running were placed under the horse's feet and hempen ropes tied round its neck ... Boys and unwedded girls sang hymns around it, happy in the hope that the very touch of the ropes would bring them luck. The brute climbed on; then sank menacingly to rest right inside Troy.

Virgil *Aeneid* 2, 229-240
(trans. Jackson Knight)

The moment when the Trojans begin the fearful act of hauling the horse into the city was sketched by a Roman painter, whose enthusiasm may have somewhat outrun his skill (Fig. 99). The wooden horse, at the right, though bigger than an ordinary horse, seems a rather modest construction, not very much larger than the humans who tug at it, dragging it inevitably toward the city. It

99. The Wooden Horse brought into Troy, Roman wall painting, about AD 50-79, Naples, Museo Nazionale, from Pompeii.

is equipped with a tower-like howdah on its back and is shown to be a *wooden* horse by the fact that its feet rest on a wheeled platform, making it look rather like a child's pull-toy. The inadequacies of the painting are compensated for, to some extent, by the liveliness of the scene, enhanced by the strong play of light on the parallel diagonals of the men pulling at the horse. A statue of Athena can be glimpsed within the city to the left. Elsewhere, orderly groups are contrasted with excited individuals. Two such agitated figures converge dramatically on the space in front of the horse, a third rushes away in the background, a fourth falls to her knees before the statue and a fifth runs out of the picture toward us. Battlemented walls loom in the background.

With the horse inside the citadel and the Greeks apparently departed, the Trojans rejoiced. They decked their temples with festive greenery, danced, sang and drank and finally, for the first time in years, fell into a deep untroubled sleep.

But, as the night wore on, fate closed its grip on the doomed city. The wooden horse was, in fact, no empty offering to the goddess. The huge hollow belly concealed the very pick of the Greek warriors and Sinon's story was a clever lie devised to deceive the Trojans and to lure them into doing just what they had done.

The Roman painter showed the wooden horse as it appeared to the Trojans (Fig. 99). But an earlier Greek artist wished to do more than that. He wanted to reveal to the viewer what in fact was concealed

100. The Wooden Horse, with the warriors that it conceals revealed (and other warriors), Greek clay relief storage vessel, about 670-650 BC, Mykonos, Museum.

from the Trojans. He did this with a certain naïve charm (Fig. 100). He portrayed the over-large horse with its feet mounted on wheels to indicate that it was an artificial construction. He cut seven square windows into the body of the horse and showed the heads of seven bold warriors framed within the windows, in order to convey the idea that the wooden horse was filled with the flower of the Greek army. Other warriors appear all around the horse. These warriors allude to what happened next.

Although the Greeks had burned their camp, they had not gone far. They anchored behind the nearby island of Tenedos and waited there for a signal to return. While the city slept, Sinon released the men hidden within the horse and gave the signal. The rest of the Greeks sailed back to the Trojan shore, advanced unhindered into the citadel and fell upon the unwary citizens.

*

Up until this moment Greek had met Trojan in armed combat. It was a fair fight. Now it simply became a massacre. There was nothing to stop the Greeks; the city lay open before them, defenceless.

Greek vase painters sought a formula to convey the true horror of the sack of Troy. Many found it in a ghastly image: an old man seeking sanctuary upon an altar (where the gods should have protected him) being battered to death by a warrior who uses the body of a young child as his weapon (Fig. 101). The two victims are both non-combatants; the altar should have remained inviolate. The scene is thoroughly shocking.

As an image of the barbarity of war, the three protagonists need no names – their ages and their situations say it all; nevertheless, within the context of the Trojan legend, these three figures are not anonymous. Even without inscriptions we can safely identify them: the old man is

101. Neoptolemos uses the body of the infant Astyanax as a weapon with which to batter Priam who has taken refuge on an altar, Attic black-figure amphora, about 550 BC, by the Persephone Painter, London, British Museum.

Priam, the warrior is Neoptolemos and the infant is Astyanax, Hektor's child.

It was generally agreed that Neoptolemos slew Priam. In the course of the war Achilles had killed Hektor; now with a certain brutal symmetry the son of Achilles killed the father of Hektor. Priam had taken refuge at an altar, and most literary sources agree that Neoptolemos actually killed him on the altar (as the vase painters liked to show) or dragged him away from it. Neither action was pardonable. This picture of the bloodthirsty, compassionless Neoptolemos slaughtering the helpless old man during the sack of Troy is very different from the noble and sympathetic Neoptolemos created by Sophokles in his *Philoktetes*. Such was the malleability of mythological heroes that diametrically opposed interpretations of their characters could be presented by different artists (or, sometimes, even by the same artist).

Astyanax, Hektor's beloved son, was still only a baby when Troy fell, but the Greeks were persuaded that he should not be permitted to survive lest he avenge the Greek destruction of his city. In Euripides' tragedy *The Trojan Women*, Hekabe denounces this cruel decision, demanding of the victorious Greeks:

> '... why did you fear this child and add slaughter to slaughter? Were you afraid he might some day raise fallen Troy? Then you are cowards after all. Our city is taken. Phrygia [the kingdom of the Trojans] is destroyed, yet you were afraid of a child, a little child, though even Hektor's victories and thousands of brave men besides could not prevent our doom ...'
>
> Euripides *Trojan Women* 1158-1164 (trans. Hadas and McLean)

According to the literary tradition, Astyanax was hurled to his death from the walls of Troy. The vase painters, however, invented their own alternative tradition. Instead of showing the infant thrown down from the walls, they showed him used as an instrument of attack against his own grandfather (Figs. 101 and 102), for, had the walls been depicted on a realistic scale, the child would have been reduced to an insignificant speck. The baby is grasped unfeelingly by the ankle, upside down. This is the position in which Telephos holds the infant Orestes to threaten him (Fig. 25). It shows a callous disregard of the infant's claim to be a human being.

Thus while literature and art concur in showing Priam murdered by Neoptolemos on or near an altar, the literary and the visual traditions go their separate ways with respect to the death of Astyanax.

Employing Astyanax as a weapon against Priam produced an image rich in implications: one single, heartless blow simultaneously extinguishes both the past and the future of the doomed city.

The power of the image was well appreciated, and it was used over and over again in pictures showing the sack of Troy (cf. Fig. 102). In Fig. 101 the central trio is complemented by several subsidiary figures: anguished women at either side, a youth and a man fleeing left and right and an impassive civilian standing at the far right. In Fig. 102 the story is amplified to the left by the scene of a Greek warrior mercilessly pulling a vulnerable naked woman away from the statue of a goddess, where she has sought sanctuary.

The naked woman could simply represent a universal type of victim, like the infant and the old man, but just as we can recognise in them Astyanax and Priam, so too we can put a name to the woman and to the warrior who is about to ravish her. The woman is the Trojan princess Cassandra. Her nakedness gives a clue to her fate; she is going to be raped. The rapist is a hero called Ajax, often referred to as 'the lesser Ajax'. The greater Ajax, whose father was Telamon, did not live to see the sack of Troy. The lesser Ajax, whose father was Oileus, disgraced the Greeks (and antagonised the goddess Athena) by dragging Cassandra away from the goddess's statue which she had assumed would protect her.

The rape of Cassandra was an eloquent image which long served as emblematic of the sack of Troy, but once a formula for the episode had been securely established (Figs. 102 and 112), artists were free to manipulate it as they saw fit. They sometimes did so in unexpected ways. For instance, a South Italian vase painter who fully appreciated the value of the conventional image chose to paint his own version of the rape – in parody (Fig. 103). The surviving fragment of his vase shows an astonished temple attendant (to the right) coming upon a *Greek warrior* clinging desperately to the statue of Athena, while a *female hand* (attached to a partially preserved female figure) is vigorously tugging at his helmet, obviously intent on having her way with him – by main force if necessary.

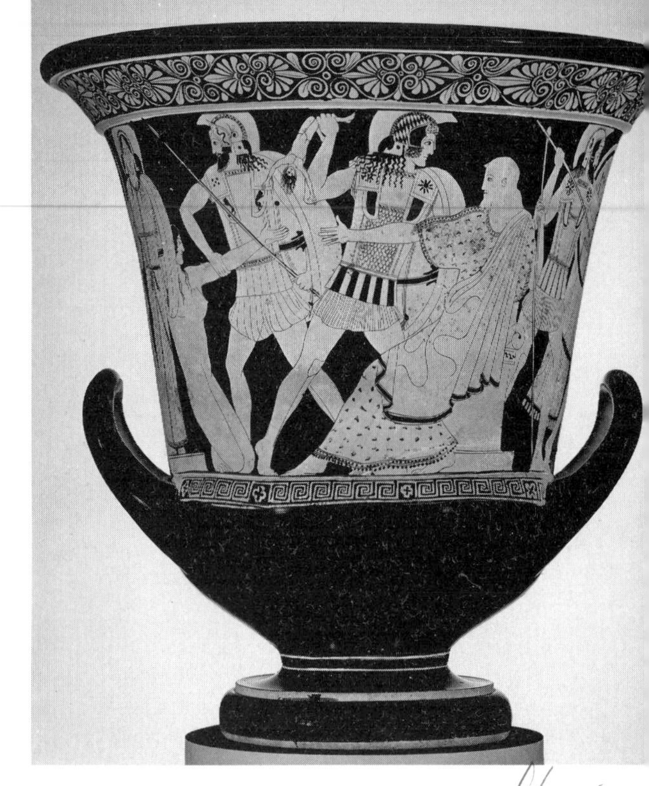

102. Neoptolemos uses the body of the infant Astyanax as a weapon with which to batter Priam who has taken refuge on an altar; Ajax, son of Oileus, drags Cassandra away from the statue of Athena at which she sought sanctuary, Attic red-figure krater, about 465 BC, by the Altamura Painter, Boston, Museum of Fine Arts (William Francis Warden Fund).

103. Ajax, son of Oileus, clings to the statue of Athena, while a sex-starved female tries to drag him away, Paestan red-figure krater fragment, about 350-340 BC, by Asteas, Rome, Villa Giulia.

104. Ajax, son of Oileus, drags Cassandra away from the statue of Athena, Roman painting in Pompeii (House of the Menander), 1st century AD.

Most artists, however, took the plight of Cassandra seriously and made eloquent use of the conventional image of her rape to conjure up some of the horrors that befell a fallen city. It was appreciated by Roman wall painters as well as Greek vase painters. Fig. 104 is one of three paintings illustrating the fall of Troy decorating a room in a Pompeian house – the other two show Laocoon and the Wooden Horse. Cassandra is portrayed clinging to the statue with one hand, her drapery slipping down her body, while the armed warrior pulls at her other arm. According to one tradition, Ajax, son of Oileus, tugged so hard that the statue was actually wrenched from its base.

Priam, Astyanax and Cassandra all represent archetypal kinds of victims – the helpless non-combatants, old men, young children and defenceless women, who suffer most in the sack of a city – but the fact that they have names and histories personalises their stories and their fates. Thus the untimely death of little Astyanax pains us more than the death of an anonymous child, for we have been touched by Homer's tender portrayal of what this baby meant to his parents and the high hopes that they had cherished for him (p. 70).

*

Priam, Astyanax and Cassandra all suffered from warriors having run amok, killing and raping in hot blood. One last horror still remained: murder committed in cold blood. According to tradition, dead warriors required satisfaction as much as live ones. For, when everything seemed to be settled, the morning after the night of slaughter, when the Greeks were preparing to set off home with their booty, the ghost of Achilles demanded his share of the sacked city. What he wanted was the sacrifice of the beautiful virgin Polyxena, daughter of Priam and Hekabe, whom once in life Achilles may have loved. The victorious Greeks dared not deny the posthumous request of their great hero. No reasonable argument, no touch of human compassion could save the guiltless maiden from this pointless death.

An Athenian black-figure vase painter has shown how Polyxena's throat was cut over the tomb of Achilles (Fig. 105). Three bold warriors hold the girl's rigid body while Neoptolemos with matter-of-fact cruelty plunges the knife into her neck.

Thus the expedition which began with the sacrifice of an innocent Greek virgin,

105. Neoptolemos sacrifices Polyxena at the tomb of Achilles, Attic black-figure amphora, about 570-560 BC, one of the painters of the Tyrrhenian Group, London, British Museum.

106. Menelaos threatens Helen, while Aphrodite protects her, Attic red-figure hydria, about 480 BC, by the Syriskos Painter, London, British Museum.

Iphigeneia, concluded with sacrifice of an equally innocent Trojan one.

*

Not everybody was killed when Troy was sacked. The devastatingly beautiful Helen was justly frightened of what her fate would be once the city fell. In fact, Menelaos hunted her out, fully intending to kill her.

A red-figure vase painter leaves no doubt as to Menelaos' intentions when he shows the aggrieved husband driving his errant wife before him, with his sword drawn menacingly (Fig. 106). Helen extends one imploring hand toward Menelaos; another woman stands at the far right. Helen seems to be fleeing into her arms. The gesture of this woman appears to be a protective one and it is probable that she is meant to be Aphrodite. Aphrodite never forgot her own role in determining Helen's fate, and she continued to feel responsible for her. In this moment of crisis, therefore, Aphrodite made use of her special powers to protect Helen, for she contrived that Menelaos somehow caught a glimpse of Helen's breasts, and so smitten was he by that seductive sight that his sword simply fell from his hand (Figs. 107 and 108). It was not long before a reconciliation was effected.

The red-figure vase painter of Fig. 108 has made all the details of the story very clear. Helen, terrified of her angry husband, has rushed to the sanctuary of an altar. Her clothes have become disordered and her beautiful body is partially revealed. Menelaos is overcome and drops the sword. His mind has turned to other matters. This is unmistakably the work of Aphrodite.

The painter of Fig. 107 is less explicit in showing the cause of Menelaos' change of heart. Helen flees to the right, holding up her skirt, but hardly more than an ankle and an elbow could be glimpsed by the pursuing Menelaos. Nevertheless his

107. Menelaos drops his sword, dazzled by Helen's beauty, Attic red-figure amphora, 475-450 BC, by the Altamura Painter, London, British Museum.

sword falls from his hand. Viewers would have known the story and could have filled in the details for themselves. The falling sword was clue enough.

Notice that the painter of Fig. 107, like the painter of Fig. 106, includes two women in the scene. The second woman on Fig. 107, who flees to the left, is unlikely to be Aphrodite, who would have a more commanding presence. She is probably just intended to be an anonymous Trojan woman, alarmed at the sight of the man with the sword. For the artist, she serves to balance Helen on the other side. In comparing Figs. 106 and 107 one can appreciate the different factors that influence an artist's arrangement of three figures, one male and two female. The artist of Fig. 106 seems more committed to telling the story and differentiating the two women; the artist of Fig. 107, by contrast, is more interested in producing a balanced composition. The two women are practically mirror images of one another: both rush away from the centre but turn their heads back and raise one hand towards the warrior between them. Only the dropped sword gives the clue that the woman on the right is Helen.

Vase painters illustrating myths were sometimes more concerned with composing well-balanced images that would effectively decorate their vessels than with producing meaningful interpretations of traditional stories. We have seen the same sort of phenomenon in Fig. 50, where the painter has doubled the fleeing Polyxena for the sake of symmetry and in Fig. 86, where the painter has given Thetis wings so that she can better balance Eos.

Helen was one of the few people who came out of the sack of Troy well; Aeneas was another. Both escaped thanks to Aphrodite's influence; the goddess had her work cut out looking after her protégés as the city fell. Aeneas was her own son and a brave man. He fought valiantly even while the Greeks were roaming the city, murdering old and

108. Menelaos drops his sword, dazzled by Helen's beauty, Attic red-figure krater, about 440 BC, Toledo, Ohio, Toledo Museum of Art.

young. According to Virgil, when Aeneas came upon Helen hiding in fear amidst the devastation, his anger rose within him and he was sorely tempted to kill the woman who was the author of so much suffering, but his mother Aphrodite restrained him, saying:

> 'Son, how can any bitterness awake in you such ungovernable fury? Why this blind anger? And how can your love for us have passed so far from your thoughts? Ought you not first to see where you have left Anchises your age-wearied father, and whether your wife Creusa and your son Ascanius still live? Around them everywhere the hordes of Greeks are prowling, and, if my thought for them had not been their defence, they would now have been caught by the flames and devoured by the pitiless sword. You must not blame the hated beauty of the Spartan Tyndarid [Helen], or even Paris. It was the gods who showed no mercy; it is they who are casting Troy down from her splendour and power .... Son, make your escape and flee ...'
>
> Virgil *Aeneid* 2, 594-629
> (trans. Jackson Knight)

109. Aeneas flees from Troy accompanied by his wife and child, carrying his father, Attic black-figure amphora, about 520-510 BC, by the Antimenes Painter, Tarquinia, Museo Nazionale.

And so Aeneas returned to his home to rescue his loved ones. Then, accompanied by his wife and little son, carrying his aged father on his back, Aeneas made his escape from the burning city. One vase painter (Fig. 109) shows Aphrodite (at the far left) protectively seeing her son off, while Aeneas, bent under the weight of his father, strides away to the right. He is preceded by his wife carrying a little child and a (nameless) archer wearing a pointed hat of the sort that was thought characteristic of Trojans (see Fig. 50).

The image of Aeneas piously carrying Anchises to safety much impressed black-figure vase painters and they delighted to represent it (see Fig. 37), often as the centrepiece of their decoration (Fig. 109). The painter of Fig. 110 has done this, but rather unthinkingly he has flanked the central group with decorative figures in mirror image. Two women seemingly dance away from Aeneas, looking back at him. The one to the right resembles the conventional figure of his wife preceding him, but the one to the left is a meaningless piece of decoration, a woman perversely fleeing in the wrong direction. Even the child appropriately placed to the right of Aeneas, between his two parents, is doubled, for another child is drawn behind Aeneas, between him and the other woman. Here the artist's sense for decoration has overruled his concern for meaningful narrative. We have seen this before, in Figs. 50, 86 and 107. The picture is markedly successful in terms of decoration, but more ridiculous than most in terms of the story. The tension between decoration and narration is a very real one for vase painters, and some are better at resolving it than others.

While the black-figure painter of Fig. 110 was ready to sacrifice meaning for decorative effectiveness, the red-figure painter of Figs. 111-112 was able to produce a beautiful and finely drawn piece of work which is, at the same time, one of the most moving representations of the sack of Troy ever created.

The decoration runs around the curved

110. Aeneas flees from Troy, carrying his father on his shoulders, accompanied by his wife and child (with other figures making for a symmetrical composition), Attic black-figure amphora, about 520-500 BC, by one of the painters of the Leagros group, Munich, Antikensammlungen.

111. The Sack of Troy: the death of Priam. Attic red-figure hydria shoulder (right side), about 490-480 BC, by the Kleophrades Painter, Naples, Museo Nazionale.

shoulder of a water jar, above the two horizontal handles. It is interrupted only at the back by the vertical handle. The very centre of the scene is occupied by the pathetic figure of Priam, seated on an altar, the image of despair (Fig. 111). He is already wounded and blood flows from his head and his shoulder. A young Greek warrior with fine features (this must be Neoptolemos) places his hand on Priam's shoulder. This is not a gesture to comfort him, but rather to steady the old man so that the youth can deliver the final blow. Priam raises his hands to his head. He is not trying to protect himself; the gesture is simply one of hopelessness and grief. Upon his lap lies the mangled body of his infant grandson, Astyanax. The child's body is horribly gashed and bleeding. It looks as if it had been violently thrown onto the old man's knees. To the right of Priam, on the ground, lies the body of a dead Trojan. To the right of Neoptolemos, a fully armed Greek crouches before the bold attack of a lightly clad Trojan

112. The Sack of Troy: the rape of Cassandra and the escape of Aeneas (left side of Fig. 111).

woman, who raises her household implement courageously against his sword. To the left of Priam, a palm tree bows in sympathy with the sufferings of the city. A woman, a captive, about to become a slave, sits beneath it beating her head. Another woman faces her, seated on the base of the statue of Athena (Fig. 112). The statue of Athena is armed and helmeted. Its spear is aimed at the Greek to the left (Ajax, son of Oileus) and under its shield, Cassandra cowers, exposed and defenceless. Ajax has grasped her by the hair to pull her away. Cassandra turns her head to face him and extends one eloquent, pleading hand toward him. A dead Trojan lies at Ajax's feet. Tragic though these images are, there is, nevertheless, a gleam of hope: at the far left Aeneas carrying his aged father on his shoulders and guiding his little son in front of him makes good his escape from the flaming wreckage of Troy. Yet even as they flee, all three look back sadly at the fallen city, its legendary splendours now no more than a memory.

Epilogue

The story of the Trojan War did not end with the sack of the city. The subsequent adventures of the survivors were recounted in the *Nostoi* (Returns), one of the books in the epic cycle, and in Homer's *Odyssey*. These events, which were retold and elaborated throughout classical antiquity, are briefly as follows.

After sacrificing Polyxena on the tomb of Achilles, the Greeks prepared to leave Troy, taking their booty with them. They had intended to punish Ajax, son of Oileus, for offending Athena by violently tearing Cassandra away from her statue, but when Ajax sought sanctuary at the very same statue, they let him go. This angered the gods, who punished the Greeks for their impiety by sending violent storms to impede their voyage home.

Menelaos and Agamemnon quarrelled before setting out from Troy, Menelaos being eager to leave at once, while Agamemnon thought it wiser to stay and try to appease Athena with sacrifices. Agamemnon may well have been right, for despite the storms sent by the angry gods, he arrived home quickly and safely, bringing the slightly deranged Cassandra along with him as part of his share of the spoils. And then his problems began.

Klytaimnestra, mourning the loss of Iphigeneia, had come to hate Agamemnon. Upon his return, she welcomed him initially with apparent cordiality but then, with the aid of the lover she had taken, murdered him. Years later, her son Orestes avenged his father's death by killing her.

Orestes was haunted by avenging Furies sent by the ghost of his slain mother. He tried several forms of expiation, was acquitted in a trial at Athens, but only found peace when, following a divine command, he fetched a statue of Artemis away from the land of the barbaric Taurians. Greeks who visited this land (on the Black Sea coast) were customarily sacrificed to the goddess by her priestess. This fate was about to overtake Orestes when it was discovered that the priestess was his long-lost sister Iphigeneia. Artemis had rescued Iphigeneia when she was about to be killed at Aulis (p. 36) and had swept her off to the land of the Taurians, where throughout the course of the Trojan war she had obediently carried out her duties at the temple. Once Orestes and Iphigeneia had recognised each other, they devised a way in which they could both abduct the statue and make good their escape.

Menelaos was caught in the storms sent by the angry gods. After much buffeting at sea and some visits to ports in the eastern Mediterranean, he finally landed in Egypt where he remained for several years accompanied by Helen, whom he had captured on the night of the sack of Troy. The alternative tradition which claimed that Helen herself had never gone to Troy – a phantom in her shape having been the cause of the ten years' fighting – maintained that the real Helen had been in Egypt all the time, and was now recovered by her husband. Whether she had been in Egypt or in Troy, Helen never lost her composure and returned to Greece beside Menelaos where she presided over his household with poise and charm.

The ship of Ajax, son of Oileus, was struck by lightning, but Ajax himself scrambled to safety. When he boasted that he had escaped without the aid of the gods, Poseidon split the rock he stood on and he drowned.

Neoptolemos, advised by his grandmother Thetis, had burned his ships in Thrace and followed a land route to arrive at his destination, taking the captive Andromache, his prize of honour, with him. Later he married Hermione, the daughter of Helen and Menelaos. This childless and unhappy union came to an abrupt end when Neoptolemos was killed by Orestes. Orestes had previously been promised the hand of Hermione and claimed her after the death of Neoptolemos.

Odysseus' homecoming was long delayed. His adventures included encounters with giants, monsters, seductively singing sirens, amorous nymphs and goddesses, and even a visit to the land of the dead. Only after twenty years' absence did Odysseus' guile, caution and intelligence enable him to recover his kingdom, his home, his wife and his son. Homer portrays Odysseus in a positive light, but later authors often had a more ambivalent attitude toward the hero. Sophokles depicted Odysseus as generously noble in his *Ajax* but as heartlessly opportunist in his *Philoktetes*. Roman authors often painted a particularly negative picture of Odysseus, whom they called Ulysses. The changing attitudes toward Odysseus and the different ways in which he was characterised provide a vivid insight into the flexibility of Greek mythology and the creative reinterpretations that were always available to artists.

Few Trojans could hope for a happy ending to their stories. Surprisingly, Andromache, who in the course of the war had suffered the tragic loss of her husband and baby, after the murder of Neoptolemos married a fellow captive, who happened to be another son of Priam's. Together they ruled over a kingdom in Epirus, where they preserved the memory of once glorious Troy.

Aeneas also eventually prospered. According to the most prevalent tradition, the one immortalised by Virgil in the *Aeneid*, his travels finally took him to Italy. The city of Rome was supposedly founded by his descendants, and this idea made the legend of Troy particularly dear to the Romans.

The fame of Troy, of course, lived on beyond antiquity and into our own day, but let the last word be spoken by Agathias, a Byzantine poet living in the 6th century AD, a time when the flame of Greek creativity had been reduced to little more than a flicker:

> O City, where are the once proud walls, the temples
> Heavy with riches? Where are the sacred heads
> Of oxen slain at the altars? Where
> Are the Paphian's [Aphrodite's] precious jars and her golden cloak?
> Where is the image of your own Athene?
>
> Gone, gone, lost to War and Time,
> And to bleak Fate, reverser of happy fortunes,
> And to harsh Envy.
> But the name of Troy
> And the glory of Troy shall live to see these die.
>
> *The Greek Anthology* 9, 153
> (trans. Fitts)

113. Helen and Klytaimnestra, when they were still young girls living at home, before their marriages and all the troubles ensued. Helen is seated at the left beside a wool basket. Klytaimnestra approaches her holding out an *alabastron* (a perfume vessel). A handled mirror hangs on the wall between them. Attic red-figure pyxis, about 460 BC, by a follower of Douris, London, British Museum.

Appendix

The Illustrations in Historical Perspective

Up to now many examples of Greek and Roman art depicting episodes in the Trojan legend have been discussed, but there has been no attempt to put these works into chronological order or to trace the development of art in classical antiquity. The purpose of this appendix is to place the heterogeneous collection of objects we have been looking at within an art historical perspective.

The illustrations in earlier chapters are hardly representative of Greek and Roman art as a whole. Some media lend themselves better than others to the portrayal of myths, and some periods encouraged the representation of myths more than others. For those interested in a more comprehensive and general view of the history of Greek and Roman art, a selection of books for further reading is given on p. 130.

Vase painting, painting and mosaics

Although painting was an accomplished and much admired art in classical antiquity, only a small percentage of the immense amount of Greek pottery and Roman wall painting that was produced survives to our day, and Greek mural and panel paintings, once highly influential, have disappeared virtually without trace.

The earliest surviving examples of Greek painting are paintings on vases. At first the decoration of vases consisted only of abstract, geometric patterns. During the 8th century BC human figures and even whole scenes began to appear. These were painted in dark silhouette on the lighter surface of the vase. It is not clear whether such early figured scenes were simply generic or whether some of them were intended to illustrate particular myths.

In the course of the 7th century BC many artists found ways to make mythological illustrations unambiguous either by selecting unique and unmistakable events for representation or by adding explanatory inscriptions. At this point, too, the technique of vase painting became more complex, some figures being drawn partially in outline and others articulated by incisions scratched into the paint before firing.

The application of incisions to the black silhouettes was the decisive factor in the creation of the 'black-figure technique' (p. 59), which was invented in Corinth at the beginning of the 7th century BC and soon adopted by the rest of the Greek world. It flourished particularly in Athens during the 6th century BC.

The introduction of incision was an important innovation, for it allowed figures on vases to remain decoratively effective while permitting them to take on subtler expressions and engage in more complex interactions. Incisions gave definition to eyes and mouths within faces, muscles on nude bodies and clothing on draped figures. They could also be used to distinguish overlapping figures from one another. The figures themselves were flat, with the parts normally shown either in full profile or full front view – heads and legs normally in profile, chests and eyes in front view; transitions were largely ignored.

Although the essence of the black-figure technique resided in silhouettes articulated by incision, the technique also admitted the addition of some colours, at first a dark purplish-red and later also white. Such added colours could make black-figure vases delightfully cheerful in appearance (e.g. Fig. 8). The colours were restricted, however, to those which could be made out of the clay slips used for painting vases and which were, therefore, suitable for firing.

During the last third of the 6th century BC, Athenian vase painters began to experiment with new techniques; they began to make use of a white ground (a white slip painted over the natural orange colour of the vase) decorated either in normal black-figure or in outline (Fig. 72). Some also experimented with a reversal of the black-figure technique, painting the background black and leaving the figures in the natural red-orange of the clay, thus creating the 'red-figure technique' (pp. 61-2).

The red-figure technique developed into something which was not simply a negative image of black-figure, for the internal markings on figures could no longer be made by means of incisions scratched into the wet paint, but had to be painted on with the aid of a flexible brush. This encouraged (or was encouraged by) a new interest in details of anatomy (e.g. Fig. 68) and in more dramatic foreshortenings (e.g. Fig. 79). Twists and turns of the body and intermediate angles were investigated and represented with increasing plausibility (e.g. the back view in Fig. 85); drapery could be shown with an abundance of soft folds (Fig. 2) and could also be used to suggest movement (Fig. 29). The addition of purplish-red gradually went out of fashion and white was abandoned early, to be reintroduced only in the 4th century BC along with touches of gilding and some fugitive colours (Fig. 3).

In red-figure, facial expression could be refined, and the drawing of an eye in profile could give direction to a glance (Fig. 23). Of course great expressiveness could be obtained by outstanding black-figure artists like Kleitias and Exekias (e.g. Figs. 90 and 94), but emotional subtlety was generally easier to achieve in red-figure.

Up until the invention of red-figure, vase painting and painting on walls and panels had differed only in the fact that a wider range of colours was always available to painters on walls and panels whose works did not have to withstand the heat of firing in a kiln. Although figure drawing continued to remain much the same in both, during the 5th century BC mural painters began to explore spatial effects that were possible when figures were shown against a light ground but which could not be produced by red-figure vase painters, whose convention required a black background.

Some of these spatial effects appear to have been explored by Polygnotos of Thasos, a celebrated mural painter of the second quarter of the 5th century BC. Before his time a single ground line had been used for all figures. Polygnotos, however, set his figures at different heights, which suggested that they were placed at different points within a spatial ambience. To call the setting a 'landscape' would be overstating the case in which a rock, a tree or a flower was often the only hint of natural surroundings. Yet figures set at different heights, with some of them partially obscured by hills or boulders, must indeed have made it appear as if some were further away (or higher up) than others. This sort of innovation is reflected in vases like Fig. 10, which also show how any suggestion of space is negated by the black background.

Though many beautiful and moving

works continued to be produced in red-figure vase painting, from about the middle of the 5th century BC it no longer attracted the very best artists and became increasing influenced by painting on walls and panels.

Red-figure vase painting continued in Athens until the end of the 4th century BC – black-figure went on, as a minor trend, even into the 2nd century BC – but vase painting was no longer representative of the most advanced ideas in painting, though it would sometimes reflect them. Figures were either arranged on a single ground line (e.g. Figs. 12 and 13) or on several levels (e.g. Figs. 10 and 45); drawing became increasingly accomplished, and sketchily drawn, broken lines (e.g. Figs. 11, 12, 45, 46) replaced the calligraphic continuous lines used in earlier times (e.g. Figs. 2, 43).

Towards the end of the 5th century BC Greek vase painters in South Italy and Sicily began to make their own red-figure vase paintings. These native schools flourished in the 4th century BC, sometimes producing somewhat bombastic works, at other times rather sentimental ones (Figs. 26 and 81) and occasionally delightfully original comic interpretations (e.g. Figs. 1, 67 and 103). Simple scenes were often arranged with figures on a single ground line (Figs. 1 and 67), more elaborate ones with figures on many different levels (Figs. 26 and 47).

Some vase painters signed their works, most did not. Many vase painters can, however, be recognised by the style of their drawing. Sometimes this is relatively easy, but at other times a trained eye combined with much painstaking labour is required if the works of a single painter are to be gathered into a coherent oeuvre. Sir John Beazley devoted a lifetime to attributing Athenian black- and red-figure vases to individual painters, giving names of his own devising (the Berlin Painter, the Kleophrades Painter, the Painter of Louvre F 118, etc.) to those whose real names were not known. A.D. Trendall has performed a similar feat in the colossal task of making order among the Greek painters who worked in South Italy and Sicily.

Painting on walls and panels, from about the second quarter of the 5th century BC, began to develop faster and along different lines from vase painting. By the end of the 4th century BC painters of walls and panels had mastered the technique of modelling in light and shadow, had discovered how to indicate the effects of highlights and cast shadows, and were able to produce works of very considerable dramatic power.

Greek painters of walls and panels during the Hellenistic period – the three centuries conventionally dated from the death of Alexander the Great (323 BC) to the final Roman conquest of the Greek-speaking world (31 BC) – had become adept not only in suggesting the massiveness of individual figures and rendering the effects of light accurately but also in placing figures convincingly within a broad landscape setting, and in creating complex compositions. They were in full possession of a sophisticated naturalistic technique which was gratefully taken over by Roman painters, whose skill (or lack of it) can best be seen in the lavish decoration of houses in the provincial towns of Pompeii and Herculaneum.

Roman wall painters drew most of their mythological illustrations from Greek prototypes of the 4th century BC and the Hellenistic period. Fig. 21 is probably a debased reflection of such a Greek prototype and Figs. 19 and 61 more dignified ones. Surviving Roman paintings of scenes from the Trojan legend seem, on the whole, to be largely dependent on Greek creations, the compositions presumably having been transmitted by means of copy-books. Nevertheless, some landscape settings which are not entirely rationally thought out and some impressionistic effects (e.g. Fig. 99) may owe more to original Roman inventions.

Mosaics composed of small, usually four-sided, pieces of coloured stone specially cut for the purpose appear to have been invented in the 3rd century BC either in Sicily or in Macedonia, though figured mosaics composed of pebbles existed earlier. The new technique proved popular not only in Greece but throughout the Roman world, at first for decorating floors and then also for walls with curved surfaces or exposed to water (like fountains or baths).

Roman mosaics representing mythological scenes seem to have drawn much of their inspiration from sources similar to those that inspired Roman paintings (Figs. 22 and 60). Copy-books were probably used as guidance for many popular narrative designs in practically all media, but certainly for mosaics. Some mosaics could be very fine and sensitive, but others degenerated into rather crude local products (Fig. 15).

Greek painting on walls and panels in the 4th century BC and the Hellenistic period had attained a high degree of persuasive naturalism and artists were able to produce works in styles similar to those found in European art from the 16th to the 19th century AD. Its influence on Roman ideas and Roman taste was immense and is reflected in the wall paintings that decorated houses in Rome, Pompeii and Herculaneum and in the mosaics found throughout the Roman world from England to north Africa and from Spain to Asia Minor.

Sculpture

There are basically two kinds of sculpture: sculpture in relief and free-standing sculpture. Sculpture in relief is similar to painting, in that figures are never cut entirely free of the background and so are viewed from the front only. The first step in carving relief sculpture was to draw the figures on the surface of the stone. The background could then be cut back behind them and the figures themselves rounded to indicate modelling. Ancient reliefs were normally painted, so that details like eyes, hair and clothing were picked out in colour and the background was made to contrast with the figures. Unfortunately the colour which once enlivened these sculptures has hardly ever survived.

The development of relief sculpture follows much the same lines as the development of painting. In the 6th century BC, figures were relatively flat and the decoration of the background was negligible. In the course of time the advances in naturalism that can be seen in painting were also applied to reliefs; anatomy was rendered more correctly and the sense of the massiveness of figures was conveyed more convincingly. By the Hellenistic period spatial settings could be suggested in relief, though this was not common.

Relief sculpture was used copiously for architectural decoration in Greece and in the Greek colonies in South Italy and Sicily (particularly for metopes and friezes). Mythological subjects were often employed, and Trojan themes were sometimes depicted, as, for instance, on some of the friezes of the archaic Siphnian Treasury at Delphi, though on the whole other stories seem to have been more popular. Nevertheless the carved metopes decorating the entire north side of the Parthenon appear to have been devoted to the Fall of Troy. Unfortunately these metopes have been so severely damaged that they are now barely intelligible and they have not, therefore, been illustrated in this book.

Relief sculpture was also used for other decorative purposes in the Greek and Roman worlds (Figs. 20 and 33). From about the middle of the 2nd century AD wealthy Romans began to choose to be buried in sarcophagi, carved marble coffins. Mythological subjects were popular on sarcophagi (e.g. Fig. 82). Artists decorating them were often more interested in producing an overall pattern through the play of light and shade than in creating a plausible vision of reality. Thus in sarcophagi such as Fig. 82 there is no consistency of scale applied to all the figures or any sense of natural space, but the whole surface is covered from top to bottom by the lively play of forms with no gaps left unfilled.

Relief was also used for the decoration of metalware (Fig. 78) and often in inverted form (that is, sunken) for the decoration of gems (Fig. 14). Vessels were also occasionally decorated with reliefs instead of being painted (Fig. 100). The techniques are very different from the carving of reliefs in marble, but the principles of design and the development are much the same.

Most free-standing statues were made either in bronze or marble, and, like sculptures in relief, were enhanced by the addition of colour. Unlike reliefs, however, which are always attached to the background, free-standing statues had to be designed so that they were self-supporting. It is easier to ensure that a free-standing statue is stable in bronze (which has considerable tensile strength) than in marble (where much care has to be taken to ensure that heavy, extended limbs are properly supported). Such structural considerations placed limitations on the kinds of poses which could be explored in different media.

The fascinating development of free-standing sculpture occupies much space in general books on the history of ancient art. They trace the development from stiff, rather schematic figures to figures naturalistically modelled and standing in a variety of free and easy poses. But as isolated free-standing sculptures only rarely convey a story, they are absent from this book.

Statuary groups, however, often embody greater narrative content (Figs. 41, 69 and 98). Groups of statues were used to fill the pediments (the triangular gables) at either end of a classical temple. At first pedimental sculptures were carved in relief, but by the end of the 6th century BC they were normally composed of an assemblage of free-standing statues (Figs. 41 and 42).

Pedimental sculptures were, of necessity, intended to be seen only from the front, but sometimes statuary groups independent of any architectural context were also designed to be seen from a single point of view. Thus the celebrated Laocoon (Fig. 98), though carved fully in the round, is intended to be viewed only from the front. The complicated tangle of human figures and snakes required considerable virtuoso skill in stone-carving and the piece has been extravagantly admired ever since its re-discovery in 1506. (It was probably originally designed for realisation in bronze.) Such a free-standing statuary group is, from a technical point of view, an extremely sophisticated creation, virtually unthinkable before the Hellenistic period. In some ways even more impressive is Fig. 69, a tightly knit group of figures cleverly designed to yield up interesting and beautiful compositions from a large number of different angles, a truly breathtaking achievement. The group was probably originally designed as a sculpture in bronze and then was adapted for marble when the Romans wished to have copies made.

Glossary

HISTORICAL FIGURES

Admetus, king of the Molossi, ruled during the early 5th century BC and was visited by Themistokles when he was fleeing from the Athenians.

Aeschylus produced some 82 plays during the course of the first half of the 5th century BC in Athens, of which only seven tragedies have survived in their entirety, though many of his lost tragedies were clearly influential and have left traces in art and literature.

Douris made and painted red-figure vases in Athens in the first half of the 5th century BC (see Figs. 87, 92, 93 and 96).

Euphronios made and painted vases in Athens during the late 6th and early 5th centuries BC. He was an early leading exponent of the red-figure technique (see Figs. 68 and 79).

Euripides produced some 92 plays in Athens during the course of the second half of the 5th century BC, many of them taking an innovative and revolutionary approach to the mythological tradition. Nineteen plays survive in their entirety, while the influence of much admired lost plays can be seen in surviving art and literature.

Exekias made and painted exquisite black-figure vases in Athens in the third quarter of the 6th century BC (see Figs. 54, 55, 80 and 94).

Homer is supposed to have composed the great epic poems, the *Iliad* and the *Odyssey*, in Greek, probably during the second half of the 8th century BC.

Kleitias painted black-figure vases during the first half of the 6th century BC in Athens (see Figs. 51, 52 and 90).

Leochares was a sculptor who probably worked in Athens around the middle of the 4th century BC and made an image of Ganymede abducted by the eagle.

Lucian composed satires, essays and dialogues, often of great wit, during the 2nd century AD in Greek, and travelled widely in the Roman empire.

Ovid was one of the outstanding Latin poets of the Augustan period (1st century BC – 1st century AD), who much appreciated and enriched the Greek mythological tradition.

Parrhasios was a Greek panel painter of the late 5th and early 4th centuries BC, all of whose works are lost, but who was celebrated for his use of outline to suggest volume. He wittily said he regretted on behalf of the hero that his painting of Ajax lost in a contest to Timanthes' painting of the same subject.

Pausanias travelled through Greece during the 2nd century AD and wrote an invaluable book in Greek describing many of the works of art he saw and admired.

Philostratos wrote a description in Greek of paintings that he saw during the earlier part of the 3rd century AD.

Pindar was a lyric poet who wrote in Greek during the first half of the 5th century BC.

Pliny the Elder compiled a *Natural History* in Latin in the 1st century AD which included a brief history of sculpture and painting.

Plutarch wrote biographies and a variety of essays in Greek in the late 1st and early 2nd centuries AD.

Polygnotos painted murals in Greece in the first half of the 5th century BC, all of which are now lost, and was a great innovator in expression and composition, apparently being the first to set his figures at different heights, rather than all aligned on a single ground line.

Sophilos painted black-figure vases in Athens in the first half of the 6th century BC (see Figs. 4, 5 and 75).

Sophokles wrote some 123 plays in Athens during the middle and later 5th century BC of which seven tragedies survive in their entirety.

Themistokles after leading the Greeks to victory over the Persians at Salamis in 480 BC was forced to flee from Athens and took refuge temporarily with Admetus, king of the Molossi.

Thucydides wrote a history of the Peloponnesian war in Greek during the later part of the 5th century BC.

Timanthes was an imaginative painter of the late 5th and early 4th centuries BC, none of whose works survive, but whose image of the sacrifice of Iphigeneia was much admired and whose painting of Ajax was judged superior to the painting of the same hero by Parrhasios.

Virgil was an outstanding Latin poet of the Augustan period (1st century BC – 1st century AD) who composed the *Aeneid*, an epic poem celebrating Aeneas' escape from Troy and his later travels.

Mythological characters

Achilles Greek hero, son of Peleus and the Nereid Thetis, in his youth was taught by the centaur Cheiron and was hidden among the daughters of Lykomedes. A great warrior, he was offended when Agamemnon took away his prize of honour, Briseis, and withdrew from the fighting until his friend Patroklos was killed. He avenged the death of Patroklos by killing Hektor and then went on to kill Penthesilea and Memnon, finally meeting his death at the hands of Paris and Apollo. Father of Neoptolemos.

Aeneas Trojan hero, son of the goddess Aphrodite and the Trojan Anchises. He accompanied Paris when he went to Greece to abduct Helen, fought bravely during the war and escaped during the sack of Troy, eventually migrating to Italy, where his descendants founded Rome.

Agamemnon Greek hero, who led the expedition against Troy to recover Helen. Elder brother of Menelaos, husband of Klytaimnestra, he sacrificed his daughter Iphigeneia for a favourable wind at Aulis. He offended Achilles by taking away his prize of honour, Briseis, and finally met his death at the hands of his wife after he had returned home.

Ajax, son of Oileus Greek hero who during the sack of Troy dragged Cassandra away from the statue of Athena at which she had sought sanctuary.

Ajax, son of Telamon Greek hero, massive in size and strength, cousin of Achilles. Vase painters showed him playing a game with Achilles and carrying his body out of battle. He fought an indecisive single combat with Hektor and finally committed suicide after losing the armour of the dead Achilles to Odysseus.

Anchises Trojan prince who was beloved of Aphrodite and, by her, father of Aeneas.

Andromache wife of the Trojan hero Hektor and mother of his son Astyanax.

Anios Greek king of Delos whose daughters could supply unlimited quantities of wine, grain and olives.

Antenor Trojan elder, friend of Priam.

Aphrodite Greek goddess of love, mother of Aeneas by Anchises, partial to the Trojans.

Paris won her favour by awarding her the golden apple. Also called 'Cypris' and 'the Paphian'.

Apollo Greek god who helped build the walls of Troy for Laomedon and the Trojans. He was instrumental in the death of Achilles. Twin brother of Artemis.

Ares Greek god of war.

Artemis Greek goddess who demanded the sacrifice of Iphigeneia. Twin sister of Apollo.

Ascanius son of the Trojan hero Aeneas, who escaped with his father.

Astyanax infant son of the Trojan hero Hektor and Andromache, killed during the sack of Troy.

Athena (called Minerva by the Romans) – Greek goddess, unsuccessful contender for the golden apple, enthusiastic patroness of Greek heroes. Also worshipped in Troy.

Atreus Greek father of Agamemnon and Menelaos.

Briseis captive girl allotted as a prize of honour to Achilles and temporarily removed from him by Agamemnon.

Cassandra Trojan princess, a prophetess whose prophecies were never believed. She was dragged away from the statue of Athena where she sought sanctuary during the sack of Troy by Ajax, the son of Oileus, and later allotted to Agamemnon, with whom she was killed by Klytaimnestra.

Cheiron learned and benign centaur who was tutor to many heroes, including Achilles.

Chryse Greek goddess of a sanctuary near Troy. Herakles sacrificed to her, and Philoktetes guided Agamemnon's expedition to her sanctuary. There Philoktetes was bitten by a snake.

Chryseis captive girl allotted as a prize to Agamemnon, daughter of a priest of Apollo whose prayers afflicted the Greeks with a plague when Agamemnon refused to return her to her father.

Creusa wife of the Trojan hero Aeneas.

Cypris an alternative name for Aphrodite.

Deianeira Greek wife of the hero Herakles, who, through the machinations of the centaur Nessos, brought about Herakles' death.

Deidamia Greek daughter of King Lykomedes of Skyros, mother of Achilles' son Neoptolemos.

Deiphobos Trojan prince, brother of Hektor and Paris.

Diomedes Greek hero who accompanied Odysseus on many expeditions.

Dionysos Greek god of wine.

Dolon Trojan spy, killed by Odysseus and Diomedes.

Eos Greek goddess of dawn, enamoured of the Trojan prince Tithonos and mother by him of Memnon.

Epeios Greek hero who constructed the wooden horse.

Eris Greek goddess of discord, who threw the golden apple into the midst of party celebrating the wedding of Peleus and Thetis.

Eros Greek god of love.

Euphorbos Trojan hero who first wounded Patroklos.

Ganymede Trojan prince abducted by Zeus.

Hebe Greek goddess of youth.

Heimarmene Greek goddess personifying destiny.

Hekabe Queen of Troy, wife of Priam, mother of Hektor, Paris and many others.

Hektor the foremost Trojan hero, son of Priam and Hekabe, husband of Andromache, father of Astyanax and brother of Paris. He fought an indecisive single combat with Ajax, son of Telamon, killed Patroklos and was killed by Achilles.

Further Reading

Greek and Roman art

Ashmole, B. *Architect and Sculptor in Classical Greece* (Phaidon 1972)
Barron, J.P. *An Introduction to Greek Sculpture* (Athlone 1981) pb
Beazley, J.B. and Ashmole, B. *Greek Sculpture and Painting* (CUP 1966)
Boardman, J. *Greek Art* (Thames and Hudson 1985) pb
Burn, L. *The British Museum Book of Greek and Roman Art* (British Museum Press 1991) pb
Hanfmann, G.M.A. *Roman Art* (Norton 1975) pb
Henig, M. (ed.) *Handbook of Roman Art* (Phaidon 1983) pb
Kähler, H. *Rome and her Empire* (Methuen 1963)
Ling, R. *Roman Painting* (CUP 1991) pb
Maiuri, A. *Roman Painting* (Skira 1958)
Pollitt, J.J. *Art and Experience in Classical Greece* (CUP 1972) pb
Pollitt, J.J. *Art in the Hellenistic Age* (CUP 1986) pb
Ramage, N.H. and Ramage, A. *Roman Art* (CUP 1991)
Rasmussen, T. and Spivey, N. *Looking at Greek Vases* (CUP 1991) pb
Richter, G.M.A. *Handbook of Greek Art* (Phaidon 1983) pb
Richter, G.M.A. *The Sculpture and Sculptors of the Greeks* (Yale University Press)
Robertson, M. *Greek Painting* (Skira 1959)
Robertson, M. *A Shorter History of Greek Art* (CUP 1981) pb
Smith, R.R.R. *Hellenistic Sculpture* (Thames and Hudson 1991) pb
Stewart, A. *Greek Sculpture* (Yale University Press 1990)
Strong, D.E. *Roman Art* (Pelican, rev. Ling 1988) pb
Williams, D. *Greek Vases* (British Museum Publications 1985) pb
Woodford, S. *The Art of Greece and Rome* (CUP 1982) pb
Woodford, S. *An Introduction to Greek Art* (Duckworth and Cornell University Press 1986) pb

Mythological illustration

Carpenter, T.H. *Art and Myth in Ancient Greece* (Thames and Hudson 1991).
Henle, Jane *Greek Myths: A Vase Painter's Notebook* (University of Indiana Press 1973).
Friis Johansen, K. *The Iliad in Early Greek Art* (Munksgaard, Copenhagen 1967).
Scherer, Margaret R. *The Legends of Troy in Art and Literature* (Phaidon 1964).

The first two volumes of Karl Schefold's magisterial works on illustrations of Greek mythology have been translated into English:

Myth and Legend in Early Greek Art, trans. Audrey Hicks (Thames and Hudson 1966 and Harry N. Abrams USA).
Gods and Heroes in Late Archaic Greek Art, trans. Alan Griffiths (CUP 1992).

Index